GIY's

KNOW-IT-ALLMANAC

Michael Kelly & Muireann Ní Chíobháin

ILLUSTRATED BY FATTI BURKE

CONTENTS

THE GIY KEY

This is Russell Sprout.
He really wants to be in the book, but, like everyone else when it comes to sprouts, we were in two minds about whether that was a good idea. Russell tries to get into most pages. **Can you count how many times he manages to make it into the book?**

HELPING HAND	BIG WORD ALERT	GARDENER PHRASE	EXTRA MILE	LOUD
Ask an adult to help you out with this bit.	Expand your vocab with this long or Latin word!	A weird gardening word to remember.	Add the finishing touch to your recipe.	Try saying this twisty phrase ten times out loud!

Published by GIY Ireland (Activities) Ltd in 2019.
Copyright GIY Ireland (Activities) Ltd.
The moral rights of the authors have been asserted.

ISBN 978-0-9930426-2-1
Printed on FSC certified paper
The information contained in this book is intended as a general guide. Neither the publisher, authors or illustrator can be held responsible for any adverse reactions to the recipes, instructions or advice given in this book. Please pay attention to the 'Helping Hand' icon (above) which indicates where children should seek parental help with a kitchen or garden activity.

The GIY story

Maybe you're already a grower; if so, welcome back my friend. Maybe you've never grown before and you're wondering why Aunt Bernie bought you this book in the first place. Well, either way, you are now officially a GIYer! We're a group of people who believe that anyone can be a grower and that growing your own food is good for you and for the planet. Think about how proud you feel when you make something yourself: a painting, a cake, a funny. It's a great feeling, right? Well … imagine what it feels like to sow a seed and have it turn into something delish you can eat!

It all begins with a guy called Mick's life-changing encounter with a simple bulb of garlic. Mick wasn't much of a grower. In fact, he was personally responsible for the death of five bonsai trees with a collective age of 3,000 years (he's still trying to make up for that to this day).

HOW DID GIY START?

After a long day at the office, feeling a bit glum, Mick decided to go to the supermarket to buy himself something nice for dinner. He grabbed some garlic to throw it into the trolley and noticed something strange … the label said the garlic had come all the way from China. In fact, it said, 'Fresh from China'. What's this about, Mick wondered. Why China? Does garlic not grow here? Could it really be 'fresh' after travelling 5,000 miles?

'How hard can it be to grow garlic?' Mick asked. Well, basically, you stick a clove in the ground and it turns into a bulb of garlic. But on his first attempt Mick sowed the cloves upside down, and, of course, they didn't grow. Oops! He wasn't going to give up that easy, and next time around he grew fourteen of the biggest bulbs of garlic you'll ever see (well, so he says).

Boosted by his garlicky success, Mick was bitten by the GIY bug. He'd bore the pants off you about how big his garlic was and how easy it was to grow food. He wanted everyone to feel as smug ... I mean *proud* ... about growing as he was, and so he set up GIY to spread the good word about growing your own food. Mick became the poster boy for GIYing, with his own TV show and paparazzi following him to the potting shed. He literally couldn't sow a pea in peace!

Mick thinks he knows all about growing, but the big secret in GIY (we can tell you now that you're a GIYer) is that the real Know-it-All hangs out in the potting shed at GROW HQ *and his name is …*

A Letter from the desk* of
MONTY SHEDDINGTON-POTTS
Grower-in-Chief, GIY

That's me ↑

Now that we've heard the garlic story (for the millionth time), I'll take it from here Mick.

So where did my journey to becoming a legendary grower begin? I was born in ... well, let's say a long time ago, in the town of Sproutchester, England, the eldest child of award-winning Brussels sprout growers Cyril and Cybil Sheddington-Potts. They gave me a lifelong love of growing and a love/hate relationship with the humble sprout: love to grow them, hate to eat them.

I showed early promise. By the age of three, I could tell my cabbages from my cauliflowers, my potatoes from my parsnips, and my radishes from my rhubarb. At age five, my father gave me my first seed tin and his battered grower's almanac. I still remember the joy of opening the tin for the first time – it was a veritable treasure trove, promising untold adventures. What were these exotic sounding seeds with weird sounding names – brassicas, umbellifers, legumes? What would they grow to look like? What on earth is chitting and surely you need a pot for that? Lots for me to learn. Lots for me to know. It was time for me to be initiated into the Sheddington-Potts' Growing Hall of Fame. It's always been a family tradition to enter the first-ever sprout you grow into the National Golden Sprout Awards, to prove you have the green fingers that run in the family.

I took the challenge very seriously, of course, the family honour to uphold. Not only did I win, but my first award-winning sprout was like no other the judges had seen before. They deemed it 'too sprouty for words' and 'too sproutastic to eat', and so I've kept dear old Russell Sprout as my mascot all these years.

* Potting shed

But what is an almanac?

An almanac is a book of information about weather, planting dates, sunset times and other useful information about nature. In the days before the internet search was invented, almanacs were hugely important for farmers and growers. Being the Know-It-All that I am, I've always wanted to create the ultimate GIY almanac to help other aspiring Know-It-Alls have the information they need to grow and cook it all ... so I suppose you could call it a **Know-It-Allmanac!** I hope these pages help you to get your plot sprouting soon.

me and Russell

OLD GROWER'S ALMANAC

SEED TIN

The only thing is, if you keep a sprout long enough, they can kind of sprout a mind of their own. I often misplace him, or maybe he misplaces me. Do give a shout if you see him about, or keep a sprout count of how many times you see him try to hog the page. He could be just about anywhere on these pages. He likes to think of himself as a 'Know-It-All' too, but there's only room for one of us in this book I'm afraid.

By age ten, I had won several giant marrow competitions and was growing enough vegetables to feed all seventeen of my siblings. My first job was as Head Gardener for Lord and Lady Toomey of Turnipton Abbey, where I spent many happy years. But, after winning the National Golden Sprout Award for the seventeenth year running, I knew there had to be more veg growing adventures awaiting me. So I travelled, learning to grow yacon in the Andes, wasabi in Japan and daikon in Africa, meeting some of the world's greatest growers. But wherever I went, there were strange mutterings about a garlic-obsessed grower in Ireland.

In Waterford, I discovered Garlic Mick, who turned out to be a great grower too – not because he knew it all (in fact he was more Know-It-Not than Know-It-All), but because he was more excited about growing than anyone I'd ever met. And he had LOTS of questions. I decided to put down roots at GROW HQ, to help the amazing GIY crew to spread the word about the growing and be their resident Know-It-All (as they like to call me).

Know-It-Alls have a bad reputation for taking over at table quizzes and always butting in with clever facts. The truth is that when it comes to growing, real Know-It-Alls are clever enough to know that you can actually never actually know it all at all. And the good news is that you don't need to know it all, or anything at all at all, to start growing food – just ask Mick. Now you too can learn to grow it all and know it all with GIY's Know-It-Allmanac.

Now, let's plough on.

MONTY
SHeddiNGTON-
Potts

GOLDEN SPROUT

my lucky
PLANT POT

JANUARY

New Year, new resolutions, and we all want to start the year with some new seed sowing, but *Know-It-Alls* know it's too cold and the days are too short. Your seeds won't thank you for it – keep them snug in the potting shed for now. But there's still plenty to get moving on in January, to work off those turkey and cabbage sandwiches.

1	2	3	4	5	6	7
Make New Year's resolution. Give up chocolate.	Break New Year's resolution.		Make a *new* New Year's resolution.	Take down Christmas tree … or hide it behind the couch for next year.	Women's Christmas / Nollaig na mBan in Ireland.	
8 Oh no! Back to school blues, six months to summer holidays! The countdown begins.	**9**	**10** Buy seeds.	**11**	**12** Cover up your vegetable beds to warm up the soil.	**13**	**14**
15	**16** Taste something you've never tried before.	**17**	**18** Pat a dog (only friendly ones).	**19**	**20** Use all the toilet roll in the house.	**21** Use toilet roll inserts to make plant pots (p. 7)
22 Think warm thoughts and count the days until summer.	**23**	**24**	**25** Don't throw away your crusts. Leave them out for the birds.	**26** Start *chitting* (p. 26)	**27**	**28**
29	**30** Have a hot cocoa.	**31** Give up chocolate (again!)	*Eanáir* Irish: anner	يناير Arabic: yanayir	一月 Chinese: yiyue	

AND NOW FOR THE WEATHER

January will be (usually) cold, wet and generally miserable.

Average temperatures are between 4 and 7°C.

The days are at their shortest with just eight hours of daylight. You wake up, it's dark. You go to sleep, it's dark. Basically, it's dark. A lot!

TOP TWO!

Expect lots of rain! January is one of the two wettest months.

Frost can be a problem, and sometimes snow.

Warmest conditions expected: under your duvet.

GIY LOG BOOK
(NOTHING TO DO WITH LOGS)

This month to HARVEST:
- ✓ CARROTS
- ✓ Parsnips
- ✓ Leeks
- ✓ Kale

Other jobs:
Put straw on rhubarb plants to keep them warm.

DON'T FORGET:
Don't get too excited and sow your seeds – they'll never make it in this cold ... *brrr!*

Now that you're a GIYer, you're going to need lots of pots to grow all your crop seedlings in. Toilet paper tubes can make great little starter pots for seedlings too.

GET CRAFTY IN JANUARY

HELPING HAND

Cut four slits at one end of the tube (about 2.5cm long).

Fold these together and interlock them at the bottom to make a base like a box.

Fill your tube with compost and plant your seed.

When you are ready to plant in your garden or in a bigger pot or planter, simply plant as it is and the tube will rot away.

JANUARY JOBS

Get some rotted compost, manure or seaweed onto your vegetable beds to make sure they are bursting with food for your plants when you start growing later in the year.

It's a dirty job but your spuds will thank you for it.

cheers!

If you put a load of garden waste – like leaves, grass, and old plants – in a corner of your garden, they will rot down and turn into really great food for plants.

GIYers call this lovely compost 'Black Gold' and will do anything for it. This is a great time of year to start a compost heap for turning food and garden waste into lots of lovely black gold.

CONTRACT

I, Monty Sheddington-Potts, promise to do your homework for A MONTH in return for some black gold.

HELPING HAND

Get a helping hand to order some seed potatoes so you can get

CHITTING!

Don't know what 'chitting' is? You'll know it all after reading p. 26.

GARDENER PHRASE

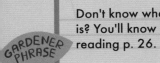

POTATOES

I ♥ 2 CHIT

HERO OF THE MONTH
CARROT

CARRATLAS

NETHERLANDS
AFGHANISTAN
ITALY
GREECE
EGYPT

The first evidence of carrot plants dates back 5,000 years to the area we now call Afghanistan. There are some ancient Egyptian drawings that depict what could have been carrots too.

In the seventeenth century, the Dutch people made the orange carrot popular by growing it in honour of their Dutch royal family, the House of Orange. Dutch people still wear orange on King's Day, in honour of their king.

The ancient Romans believed that carrots made you windy. Roman writer Diphilus even wrote about it, saying that carrots caused 'loosening and windiness'. The 'windiness' can be explained by the fact that raw carrots take a bit more effort to digest.

A VEGETABLE FIT FOR A KING!

Most of us are used to seeing orange carrots but did you know there are also purple, black, yellow and red carrots? It's thought that the orange carrot came from crossing a red and yellow carrot.

I CARROT LIVE WITHOUT YOU

The ancient Greeks believed that eating carrots helped you fall in love. They called carrots *Philtron*, meaning 'love charm'.

Ancient Romans enjoyed eating carrots raw, dressed in oil with salt and vinegar – a kind of ancient Roman slaw.

The orange carrots the Dutch grew became a popular food and travelled to England during Queen Elizabeth I's reign. Carrots were such a must-have food there that they even became a fashion accessory. People used to decorate the tops of their hats with them!

GET TO KNOW YOUR ROOTS

Carrots are what we call 'tap roots'.
This is a big, central root that grows down into the ground, helping the plant stay in place and stay stable when it's windy. Parsnips are another example of a root vegetable that we eat. Roots conduct water and food from the soil into the plant. If you want to see how roots absorb water:

⚠ SPOILER ALERT!

The green leaves will start to regrow at the top into a carrot ponytail, proving that the carrot is a root that absorbs water.

But don't get your hopes up too high, carrots are tap roots and you won't grow a full carrot this way.

Half fill a jar with water.

Cut the top off a carrot.

Put the carrot top in the jar of water and put it in a window that gets sunshine.

Watch and wait to see what happens.

CARROT MYTHS AND LEGENDS

DO RABBITS ACTUALLY LIKE CARROTS?

Not really. Rabbits don't actually eat carrots in the wild and usually prefer grass. Pet rabbits can get toothaches from eating too many carrots, so maybe offer them some grass or hay instead.

IF YOU EAT TOO MANY CARROTS WILL YOU TURN INTO ONE?

Well ... if you eat a large number of carrots, the palms of your hands can turn an orange-yellow colour. It's called *Carotenemia*.

BIG WORD ALERT

(But don't worry, it goes away if you cut back on eating too many.)

DO CARROTS GIVE YOU NIGHT VISION?

This myth was started in the Second World War by the RAF in Britain to cover up the fact that their pilots were using new radar technology when flying their planes at night. The RAF said that the pilots were seeing their targets better at night because they were eating lots of carrots which were giving them improved night vision.

Carrots are very high in 'beta carotene', which changes to vitamin A in our bodies.

Vitamin A can help your eyes' ability to adjust to light changes, but it probably won't give you night vision superpowers overnight.

BIG WORD ALERT

MONTY'S KNOW-IT-ALL → STATS ←

Carrots are made up of approximately 87 per cent water.

Carrots are from the *Umbelliferae* family, and lots of vegetables in this family look a bit like an umbrella, hence the name.

BIG WORD ALERT

Carrots are a root vegetable.

Carrots have been used in cakes since the Middle Ages when sweeteners were expensive and difficult to get. Honey was also used as a natural sweetener.

The average person who eats carrots will eat over 10,000 of them in their lifetime.

Carrots have natural sugar in them. The Celts called them 'honey underground', probably for that reason.

GROWING
CARROTS

Lots of grown-up GIYers think carrots are hard to grow. That's just because they don't know GIY's **Three-Step Program to Carrot Awesomeness ™**

TOP SECRET!

	Jan	Feb	Mar	Apr	May	Jun	Jul	Aug	Sep	Oct	Nov	Dec
Sow			✓	✓	✓	✓	✓	✓				
Harvest						✓	✓	✓	✓	✓	✓	

1   2   3

*These are fun to look at but a nightmare to peel.

Step 1

Remember, the carrot we eat is actually a root. We sow the seed and the root heads off into the soil in search of water and food. If it meets hard soil or a stone on the way down, it will stop, or fork*, in the soil. So the trick is to have soil that's nice and crumbly with no stones in it, down to about 30cm deep (the length of a big carrot). If using a container to grow carrots in, it should be at least 20–30cm deep for the same reason.

Step 2

Carrot seeds are tiny and if the soil is lumpy they can fall down into the cracks between lumps! So you need to get the soil nice and flat by raking it to what we Know-It-Alls call a 'fine tilth'.

GARDENER PHRASE

Step 3

Be patient – carrots can take up to two weeks to germinate!

SOW

A bit like myself, carrots don't like being moved once they've been sown and put down roots. So we always sow them 'direct' – either in the soil or in a deep pot or container.

NO NO WE WON'T GO

NOT MOVING

GARDENER PHRASE

When to Sow:
You can sow carrots any time from March to August, but they grow better if you wait until April when the weather's warmer.

How to Sow:
Make a little drill 2cm deep and sow the seeds in it. Cover back over with soil. If you've more than one row, keep them 20cm apart.

GROW

You will only need to water carrots in very dry weather. In fact, the drier it is the deeper the carrot root will grow looking for water! A thirsty carrot is a big carrot …

No, JUST Thirsty

wow, you're tall!

Once they have germinated and started to grow, 'thin out' until you have 5cm between seedlings.

'Thinning out' means we take out and throw away some seedlings to make sure there is enough space for the ones left behind to grow properly.

GARDENER PHRASE

5cm

HARVEST

7 WEEKS

12 WEEKS

When to Harvest:
You could have baby carrots seven weeks after sowing, about twelve weeks for bigger ones.

It's best to use a garden fork to get the carrots out. You might break them if you try to pull them out.

BASICS: SEEDS

Even though I always tell Mick that it is I, Monty, who does all the hard work in the GIY garden, really it's the seeds that do all the heavy lifting.

Since I was a boy, I've always thought that seeds are miraculous. They have everything they need inside to become a plant that will produce loads of food.

Think about this: a teeny tiny tomato seed will become a tomato plant up to eight feet tall that can produce up to 300 tomatoes!

In the winter months, in the potting shed, I've often wondered, how do tomato seeds know to become a tomato plant? What would happen if a tomato seed decided to be a rebel and become a cauliflower instead? Or a ballet dancer?

MONTY SHeddiNGTON-PottS

WHAT IS A SEED?

A seed is a tiny plant, waiting to happen. What's it waiting for? A bus? A train? A pay rise? It's waiting for the right conditions to start growing or 'germinate'.

The next time you open a seed packet think about how long those little seeds have been waiting for their chance to grow. This is their **BIG MOMENT**.

Grown-ups make growing out to be harder than it is, with all those Latin names for plants, and weird gardening words. In fact, GIYing is pretty simple. You just need **THREE SOMETHINGS:**

SOME kind of seed
(Pick a seed, any seed)

SOMEthing to sow your seed in
(like a pot or container)

SOMEthing to grow your seed in
(like soil or potting compost)

And that's it. See? Not a Latin name in sight.

Phew!

WHAT ARE THE RIGHT CONDITIONS?

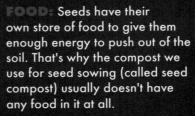

Pretend the seed is a famous, though slightly diva-like, footballer (Seedaldinio) insisting on the following conditions before it will come out of the ground:

MY DEMANDS

The right amount of water. Not too little, not too much.

The right temperature: a balmy 20°C or so.

Daily foot massage.

THINGS SEEDS DON'T NEED

FOOD: Seeds have their own store of food to give them enough energy to push out of the soil. That's why the compost we use for seed sowing (called seed compost) usually doesn't have any food in it at all.

LIGHT: Funnily enough, most seeds* don't need light until after they germinate, but once they start to grow, their leaves need light to photosynthesise and produce food for themselves.

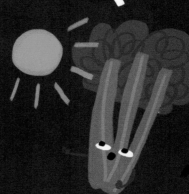

*Just to be super awkward, celery and lettuce are two types of seeds that need **light** to germinate. That's why when we

WANTED CARROT ROOT FLY

The **carrot root fly** is my favourite of all veg patch pests. It's single-minded, a bit like Mick. The flies LOVE carrots and can smell them for miles around. If the carrot root fly was a superhero, its would be its sense

The fly lays eggs at the top of the carrot which become maggots. Then these little maggots start eating the carrots. If you cover the carrots with some netting, the carrot root fly can't get at your carrots. Come to think of it it's fairly easy to thwart the it's not much

EAT

HANDY HACK FOR A CARROT STICK SNACK

Although the Romans thought raw carrots could make you a bit ... *you know* ... carrots are tastiest when they are raw. The only problem is, because carrots are mostly made of water, they can dry up quickly and aren't as nice to eat when they are dry. A handy hack is to store your chopped carrot sticks in a little water.

If you are making your snack the night before to take to your shed or school, store your carrot sticks in a sealed jar of water in the fridge overnight. In the morning, pop your carrots into your lunch box and sprinkle a little water over them before you seal it, and they'll be crunchy and juicy when snack time comes. It works for celery sticks and cucumber sticks too.

Do you like chicken wings? Ever thought of making them with cauliflower? Try this Curried Cauliflower Wings recipe I picked up from cowboy Bullhop McCabe at the Yeehaw Rodeo in Texas.

If you want to go the extra mile, squeeze the roasted bulbs of garlic into some mayonnaise and use as a dip.

EXTRA MILE

HERB HERO

The Scottish say that this soup keeps you warm, and let's face it, they'd know. They wear kilts even in winter. Practise your best Scottish accent by saying 'Cock-a-Leekie' over and over again.

WHAT'S IN January SEASON

KALE + CABBAGE
Try the super slaw on the next page.

LEEK
The Scottish national soup of chicken and leeks actually started in France as Coq-au-Leek (coq is French for a male chicken) but the Scots called it Cock-a-Leekie.

CAULIFLOWER
Cut your cauliflower into big chunks. Rub in oil, a squeeze of lemon and some mild curry powder. Roast on a tray with unpeeled bulbs of garlic for 25 minutes at 150°C.

BEETROOT
Most people eat it from a jar when it's pickled with vinegar, but I like to peel my beets, rub them in oil or butter, add a pinch of salt, wrap them in tinfoil and roast them in the oven on a medium heat for 20 minutes.

PARSNIP
Cut into chunks and roast in the oven for sweet parsnip chunky chips.

Or you can slice them thinly, spread them on a baking tray and roast them to make veggie crisps.

PARSLEY

Did you know? Parsley and carrots are actually from the same family. If you look at carrot leaves, they even look a little like parsley. Some people eat parsley to make their breath smell better – *especially* after eating garlic. Long ago, people in Ireland put parsley under beds to get rid of fleas!

When to sow? Sow seeds from May to September in a 10cm pot.

How to grow? Grow in a pot or plant out, spaced 40cm apart.

Tasty in:

PARSLEY FRESH

STUFFING

SOUP

SALAD

SAUCE

CARROT GOLDEN RULE

Never overcook a carrot! Now you are a GIYer, you must make this your solemn vow! Carrots should be **firm**, not soggy and squishy when cooked. Between 5 and 7 minutes steaming or boiling is enough to cook them and still keep the good stuff like vitamins and minerals in.

CARROT CAKE BREAKFAST BALLS

Cake for breakfast? Why not? This recipe might have been Marie-Antoinette's* favourite thing to eat for breakfast. I learnt it from a baker in Versailles, France, et voilà – les carrot cake breakfast balls.

*a cake-obsessed queen of France during the French Revolution.

Blitz a washed carrot (1 small)
Chopped dates (8)
Vanilla essence (1 tsp)
Oats (125g)
Cinnamon (1 teaspoon)
Almond or peanut butter (1 tbsp)
Walnuts (6)
or, if you are nut free:
Sunflower seeds (1 tbsp) and
Coconut oil (1 tbsp)
in a food processor until they are well mixed.

make sure the pit, that pesky seed like a stone in the centre, has been removed.

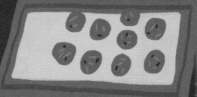

HeLPING HAND

Mix raisins (70g) into the blitzed mixture.

Cover your mixture and place in the fridge for 10 minutes to firm up.

Roll the cooled mixture into balls using your hands, place in a lunch box and cool overnight. Store in fridge until serving to keep firm. Eat within five days.

makes 12 balls

You can roll the balls in coconut flakes, crushed walnuts or crushed almonds, but remember to check that none of your friends are **allergic to nuts** before offering them some.

EXTRA MILE

The NOT-SO-GREAT POETRY CORNER

CARROT, CABBAGE & KALE SUPER SLAW

makes enough for 4

The word 'slaw' is said to come from the Dutch word *sla*, short for *salade*, meaning … well, salad.

I think you can make a slaw from just about any food that can be grated: cabbage, lettuce, carrot, even kale. Kale will never let you down in the winter months and is a sturdy plant that grows right through the coldest months of the year. It's great on a baked spud, in sandwiches or on its own. Take it with you in a box for lunch!

HeLPING HAND

Shred then tear away the tough stems from the leaves of kale (100g) with your hands. Bunch the leaves together into rolls and shred into thin strips using a kitchen scissors.

TOO CHEWY

Grate carrots (2 large)
White cabbage (200g) and
Apple (1 small eating apple, peeled and cored) into a bowl.

Caution: do mind your fingers – they are quite handy!

You can use a food processor if you happen to have one of those wonder gadgets. I quite like to do it by hand to challenge my arms to the workout.

Mix the shredded kale, grated carrot, cabbage and apple. If you'd like extra texture then you can add **raisins** (3 tbsp) and **pine nuts** (1 tbsp).

Shake, shake, shake the juice of 1 lemon
Olive oil (2 tbsp)
Apple cider vinegar (2 tbsp)
Mayonnaise (3 tbsp)
Salt and pepper (pinch) and
shredded **parsley** (handful)
together in a jar.

Cake for breakfast?

Yes please!

Pour the dressing over your kale slaw!

GARY GREENFINGERS

Why is he called Gary Greenfingers?
Because what he plants always grows?
It's a puzzle, a question that lingers
Where Gary went for a pick of his nose.

One January day at the compost heap,
Where Gary went to pick his nose,
An icy wind blew and the snow was deep.
And Gary's nose-picking finger? It froze.

He tried to remove it, by wriggling and jiggling,
The offending finger about.
But the snot-seeking, nosey finger,
Was wedged right up his poor snout.

Something had to be done, this wasn't much fun.
How would he thaw his paw out?
So he wished for some sun and in May when it shone,
His finger popped out green, like a sprout.

13

FEBRUARY

February is a mysterious month that sometimes has twenty-eight days and sometimes twenty-nine. Know-It-Alls are always ready to leap into action and look forward to every fourth year when February gives us an extra day to put a spring in our step and get sowing. Being the month of love, show your plot some tender loving care in February.

1	2	3	4	5	6	7
St. Brigid's Day in Ireland. If your name is Brigid then everyone has to do what you say today.	Groundhog Day in the USA.	Feed the birds.		Start collecting vegetable scraps and fruit peels for this month's mini composter project.		Time to get the shed in order!
8	9	10	11	12	13	14
Start spring cleaning!	Don't forget to spring clean under your bed – you never know what you'd find!		Find a plastic bottle for a mini composter project on p. 15.		World Radio Day. Blast your favourite radio station and get jobs done in the garden.	Valentine's Day
15	16	17	18	19	20	21
Pal-entine's Day. Tell your pals why you think they're great.	See what you can see in a puddle.		Invent a Smoothie Day!			International *Hug a Hedgehog* Day (OK we made that one up).
22	23	24	25	26	27	28
	See if you can make a weeping willow cry.		Make up a knock-knock joke.	Bring Your Dog for a Pedicure Day (OK we made that up too).		
29						
Leap Day! An extra day once every four years.	If you were born on the 29th of February, then you only have a birthday every four years – during a leap year. That means you should have an *extra* special birthday cake.					

이월
Korean: *iwol*

Luty
Polish: *lootay*

Únor
Czech: *oonar*

AND NOW FOR THE WEATHER
SPRING

ON MY WAY!

February is usually a cold, wet and windy month so don't put away your rain gear just yet!

But don't worry: the days are slowly getting brighter, and spring is on its way.

If you see a groundhog, ask it when it thinks spring will be here! It's said that they can tell by their shadow when spring will come.

Warmest conditions can be expected in a cup of hot chocolate or in your hot press.

-ANY DAY NOW!

Average temperatures are around 3-7°C but don't rule out snow and frost in February. Colder days haven't quite gone on their icy way yet.

GIY LOG BOOK
(NOTHING TO DO WITH LOGS)

This month to **SOW:**
- ✓ Tomatoes
- ✓ Aubergines
- ✓ Peppers

This month to **HARVEST:**
- ✓ Kale
- ✓ Spinach
- ✓ Winter Cabbage

Other jobs:
- ✓ Chit Potatoes
- ✓ Buy Seeds

GET CRAFTY IN FEBRUARY

MAKE A MINI COMPOSTER:

Take a 2 litre plastic bottle (remove labels with warm soapy water).

HELPING HAND

Get a helping hand to help you cut the very top off the bottle and punch some holes in the side and bottom of the bottle.

Place the bottle on a small plate. Put some shredded newspaper, leaves and soil from your garden in the bottom of the bottle.

Add your compost materials: grass clippings, fruit peelings and vegetable scraps. Don't add dairy or meat.

Sprinkle enough water to dampen the contents of your bottle composter.

Take the top of the bottle you cut off earlier. Turn it upside down and fit it into the top of the bottle.

Add a little water into this opening every day to make your compost rot. Cover the top of your compost with an old tea towel and keep in a safe place. Watch what happens!

SPOILER ALERT! ⚠️

You might see fluffy mould growing on it. When your compost is ready (rotted), you can use it in the garden to make your plants grow.

FEBRUARY JOBS

GIYers are always itching to get started with their seed sowing in February but one must be patient. Every year I remind myself not to be too hasty and keep an eye on the weather forecast. If it's too cold, it's better to wait until it warms up.

Tomatoes, peppers and aubergines have a long growing season, so I sow my seeds late this month. Because they need temperatures of around 20°C to germinate, I keep the seed trays or pots in the hot press beside Mrs Sheddington-Potts' favourite towels (but they would probably be better on a heated mat in the potting shed).

MONTY!!

With the short, dark days, the lack of light can be a problem for seedlings. They stretch to reach the light and become 'leggy' as a result. It might sound fun, but a leggy seedling is a weak seedling. Best to keep them on a windowsill where it's the brightest.

FOLLOW THE LIGHT

GARDENER PHRASE

February is the last chance to plant fruit trees (apple, pear or plum) or bushes (raspberries, blackcurrants). If you want to make delicious fruit smoothies, sorbets or cordials this summer, the best time to plant fruit trees and bushes is in the winter months when they are dormant.

HERO OF THE MONTH
BEETROOT

HOLD that thought!

RØØTPASTE

In ancient times, the root was used as medicine for toothaches.

The Romans, hopeless romantics that they were, believed that beetroot made you fall in love, but they also thought that beetroot was good for keeping your trips to the lavatory regular, so maybe beetroot was the food of love and of the lav in ancient Rome.

There are also pictures of beetroot on the walls of Pompeii that show beetroots as a food of love.* I give Mrs Potts a bunch of beetroots, the vegetable of love, as a Valentine's present every year. What can I say, I'm a hopeless romantic myself, but perhaps she'd prefer a bunch of flowers …

*The famous Mount Vesuvius volcano erupted in 79AD and covered the city of Pompeii in ash, preserving it as it was at that time.

BORSCHT

CWIKLA

Beetroot became popular in Eastern Europe when it began to be used in dishes like borscht. Borscht is a beetroot soup made in many countries of Eastern Europe. Poland has cwikla, which is a mix of beetroot and horseradish that people eat in sandwiches, salads and with different types of cold meats.

Not only was beetroot used for colouring food, but in the past it was used as make-up. The early Celts used powdered beetroot as blusher and lipstick, and many cultures used beetroot to dye hair.

The Pennsylvania Dutch have a tradition of making pickled beetroot eggs. The beetroot is removed from the jar of vinegar and replaced with boiled eggs which pickle and turn red. Would you eat a red egg? I know I would!

well this is embarrassing…

In Victorian times, beetroot was used as a food colouring to bring colour into their colourless diet. Adding colour to desserts made them exciting, and the beetroot was also used as a sweetener. I still love a bit of beetroot in my pudding. Would you eat a cake made with beetroot? (See my Beetroot Brownie recipe on p. 21.)

Beetroot BEAUTY

You can use beetroot juice to make your own beetroot face paint cheaply.

1 Get a helping hand to boil some peeled beetroot in water.

2 Strain the beetroot and keep the red coloured water the beets were cooked in. Allow the water to cool.

HELPING HAND

3 Mix your beetroot water dye with a little plain flour to make a paste that you can use as a face paint.

Hearty Beets

I'm sure you've tried potato painting before, but I prefer to use beetroot. I find it makes superior art to the spud because it has its own in-built ink.

1 Get a helping hand to boil a beetroot, and, when cool, cut in half and you've got yourself a beetroot stamp you can make your mark with.

HELPING HAND

2 Sometimes for Valentine's Day I cut a heart shape into the beetroot and use it to make heart stamps for Mrs Potts' Valentine's cards. You can also use the stamp on your skin as a temporary heart tattoo.

you can't beet a good card!

You can use any of the coloured water you have left from the boiled beetroot to dye sheets of paper pink or red. I might even make my Valentine's cards using my own beetroot stationery this year.

BEETROOT MYTHS AND LEGENDS

CAN YOU *REALLY EAT* EVERY PART OF A BEETROOT?
Absolutely. Know-It-Alls know that beetroot hides a secret: it's not one veg, it's actually three veg in one! You can eat every part of this amazing little plant.

Roots: This is the bit we usually eat, but they taste best if you don't let them grow too big.

Stems: The lovely bright red stems of beetroot are fantastic to eat if you chop them and fry gently in a little butter.

Leaves: Baby leaves from the beetroot plant are fantastic in a salad.

IS BEETROOT ALWAYS STORED IN VINEGAR?
Know-It-Alls have been preserving foods in vinegar for centuries. In the past, it was a clever way of storing food for long periods when food mightn't be in season or even in times of shortage because of wars.

After the Second World War, some vegetables were difficult to get because of food rations, so pickled beetroot became one of the most available vegetables in Europe and a household favourite. Pickled beetroot remains very popular for salads, but it's not the only way to enjoy beetroot.

Help! I'm shrivelling up in here!

CAN EATING LOTS OF BEETROOT TURN YOUR PEE PINK?
Some people's bodies have difficulty breaking down the betanin contained in beetroot. If they eat lots of beetroot it causes *beeturia*, ← which is when urine (pee) turns red or pink.
The only way to find out if you are someone affected by beeturia is to eat some beetroot and, well … check what happens! So, my aspiring Know-It-Alls, I challenge you to take the GIY Grand Beeturia Challenge and record your findings!

BIG WORD ALERT

MONTY'S KNOW-IT-ALL → STATS ←

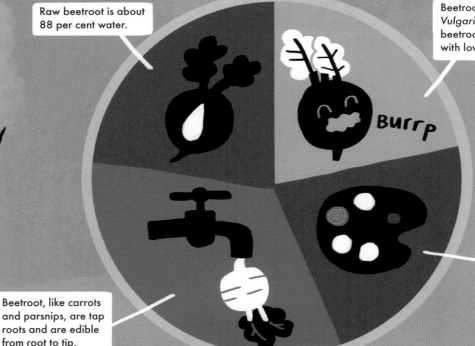

Raw beetroot is about 88 per cent water.

Beetroot is also known as *Beta Vulgaris*, but that doesn't mean ALL beetroots are vulgar. I've met some with lovely manners over the years.

BIG WORD ALERT

Burrp

Beetroot contains betanin which gives beetroot its red colour. Betanin is used as a red food colouring in many foods. You might be surprised to find that some packaged sauces get their red colour from beetroot.

Beetroot, like carrots and parsnips, are tap roots and are edible from root to tip.

GROWING BEETROOT

Lady ... they would inspect beetroot before it was allowed in to the Turnipton Abbey kitchen, so I've always been obsessed with growing perfect specimens. Thankfully, it's easy to grow if you follow the tips below.

	Jan	Feb	Mar	Apr	May	Jun	Jul	Aug	Sep	Oct	Nov	Dec
Sow		✓	✓	✓	✓	✓	✓					
Harvest						✓	✓	✓	✓	✓	✓	

Succession Sowing

Some seed packets have hundreds of seeds in them, but if you sow all the seeds at the same time, the veg will all be ready to eat at once. That's perfect if you're throwing a banquet for 500 of your closest friends, but otherwise not a great plan!

Succession sowing is where we sow a little bit every now and then so that smaller amounts of the veg are ready to eat as we need them. Beetroot is an example of a vegetable that we succession sow.

GARDENER PHRASE

To keep the GIY kitchen supplied all year round, we **sow three times a year:**

February

If your school or home has a glasshouse or polytunnel, you can sow beetroot in February which should be ready to eat in June, just in time for the school holidays.

March

Do a second sowing in March or April for a harvest that will be ready over the summer months.

July

Do a final sowing in early July which will be ready to eat in October and can be stored over winter.

SOW

Where to Sow:
You can sow beetroot seeds direct in the soil, but we always start ours in a module tray* to transplant** later.

How to Sow:
Fill the tray with compost and give it a little bang on the table to settle the compost and get rid of any air pockets.

Place one seed in each module in the tray. Push each seed into the compost about 2cm deep and cover up with some compost. Give it a water.

*A 'module tray' is one of my top Know-It-All Handy Hacks. It has little compartments in it for each seed to keep their roots apart as they grow. Think of it like a Montessori school where seedlings have space to grow and become healthy happy.

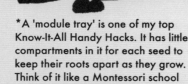

GROW

When to Transplant:
When the seedlings are large enough and ready to graduate to life outside the module tray (about four weeks) it's time to move them on to either a larger container or into the soil outside.

I don't want to leave

How to Transplant:
Plant them 10cm apart and leave 30cm between rows.

Know-It-All Handy Hack
Did you know you can store beetroot in a box of play sand for up to three months?

**Transplanting is about carefully planting out a seedling that you've started in a pot or tray (see p. 35).

see p. 35

NOT THIS TYPE OF TRANSPLANT

HARVEST

When to Harvest:
Harvest the beets when they're nice and small (somewhere between the size of a golf ball and a tennis ball) and they will taste delicious.

BASICS: Feeding Your Soil

As veg plants grow, they take the food they need to grow from the soil. Every year, we have to feed our soil to replace the nutrients that we've taken from it by growing veg that year. Think about this: since nutrients eventually end up in our bodies from the veg we eat, there is a connection between the health of our soil and our own health.

What's your favourite food? Well, for vegetables, their favourite foods are nitrogen (N), phosphorus (P) and potassium (K). They also love the extra nutrients they get from healthy soil that has plenty of organic matter in it. To make sure our soil is really healthy and the plants have lots of their favourite foods, we cover the soil each winter with a layer of either seaweed, home-made compost or farmyard manure. Yes, by manure I mean poo from farmyard animals like pigs, sheep, horses, cows or chickens. It's rocket fuel for your soil.

A good rule of green thumb for Know-It-Alls is to add a bucket of any of the above for each meter of veg bed. As they rot down, these bulky materials feed the soil and make it more crumbly. Earthworms will love it, and having lots of earthworms in the soil improves it even more, because they put little drainage tunnels in the soil as they move around.

MONTY SHeddiNGTON-POTTS

WHere Can I get these SUPERFOODS?

Seaweed
Mrs Potts and I love to collect seaweed from the beach the day after a storm

Compost
Make it yourself in a compost heap at home or school by adding layers of brown and green kitchen or garden waste and letting it rot down.

Farmyard Manure
I make friends with all my local farmers in the hope that they will give me some farmyard poo, but you can also buy it in bags in a garden centre. If you have a few hens at home or school, their ahem, you know, eh, droppings are amazing to help veg grow.

PLANT PICK-ME-UPS

Sad Plant

If you get a good layer of compost, seaweed or rotted manure on your beds in the winter, you shouldn't need to feed your plants during the year. If plants look like they need a bit of a pick-me-up, we give them a feed during the year using either a sprinkle of poultry manure pellets, a handful of dried seaweed or comfrey tea.

Happy Plant

Recipe for COMFREY TEA

HELPING HAND

Do not drink, unless you're a plant!

Leaves

Hessian sack

Water

Tight Fitting Lid

BIN

1 Cut 500g of comfrey leaves from a plant and put them in a hessian sack. Hessian is a special type of natural material made from plant fibres. It is permeable, which means it lets water in and out.

2 Put the sack in a bin and add 15 litres of water. Put on a secure lid.

3 Wait about a month. It's strong stuff so put one litre of tea into a watering can and add ten litres of water. Use it to feed plants.

Tea-RIFFIC COMFREY TEA

GARDENER PHRASE

At their tea parties, plants prefer 'comfrey tea', which is a tea made from the leaves of the comfrey plant. Comfrey is an amazing plant that has a very long tap root which mines potassium from deep in the soil. This means that a tea from its leaves is rich in potassium and great for fruiting plants like tomatoes, cucumbers and courgettes. At GROW HQ we have some comfrey plants that we just grow in order to

Note: Comfrey tea stinks so make sure your bin has a tight fitting lid! You can also m...

EAT

Celeriac is one of the ugliest vegetables, but this big knobbly turnip-shaped swollen stem is edible, closely related to celery and delicious. In fact, celeriac is one of my favourite vegetables to make chips out of.

HANDY BEET HACK
You can store beetroot in sandpit sand and it will last longer, or you can cook it and pickle it in vinegar in a jar and use it when you need it.

There are lots of different types of mushroom, but many are poisonous. Buy some local, fresh, large mushrooms and celebrate Stuffed Mushroom Day!

WARNING!
Don't pick them yourself!

Go the extra mile and serve with garlic mayo for the extra yum factor.

EXTRA MILE

HERB HERO

THYME

Get a helping hand to peel and chop your celeriac into chips, like you would with a potato, then boil for 4 minutes.

Strain them and toss them in healthy oil on a baking tray with chopped rosemary, crushed garlic, salt and pepper and a squeeze of lemon juice.

Roast in the oven at a medium heat for half an hour, until they are golden.

Get a helping hand to stuff a mushroom with chopped onion, chives, breadcrumbs, chopped tomato, chopped garlic and top it with grated cheddar cheese.

CELERIAC

MUSHROOMS

WHAT'S IN February SEASON

Did you know?
Thyme was used by the ancient Egyptians to embalm their mummies. Ancient Greeks used to burn it in temples to bring courage, and knights in the Middle Ages often carried it to battle to bring them courage and good luck. In the Middle Ages, people used it as an air freshener. They also put it under their pillows to soothe themselves to sleep and keep nightmares at bay.

Drizzle a little healthy oil over the mushroom and wrap in tinfoil. Cook in the oven on a medium heat for 20 minutes until the mushroom is juicy, the stuffing is crispy, and the cheese is melted.

SWEDE

CAULIFLOWER

It's said that a botanist crossed a cabbage with a turnip and produced a swede. Swede is also known as 'rutabaga' from the Swedish word *rutabagg*. I've heard tales that swedes were used as a cheap cannonball substitute in Britain in the 1800s! Seems like a waste of good swedes to me.

I once met a man who was a big cauliflower fan and ate it every day. Interestingly, he was also a former rugby player and had cauliflower ears. He had some spectacularly inventive ideas for how to use it, even as rice! It's quite easy and tasty.

When to sow?
You can grow thyme from seed. Sow the seed in April in module trays or pots and then plant out the little seedlings, leaving 15cm between plants.

Swede is delicious when boiled until tender and mashed with milk, butter, salt and pepper.

HELPING HAND

Make Cauliflower Rice!
Get a helping hand to blitz some cauliflower florets using the grater setting in your food processor to make something that looks just like rice. Cook in a little oil in a frying pan for 8 minutes. I like to add soy sauce to my cauliflower rice.

How to grow?
As it's a 'perennial' (grows for many years) you could buy a small thyme plant instead of growing from seed.

GARDENER PHRASE

STEW

Tasty in:

CHICKEN DISHES

STUFFING

ROAST POTATOES

Beetroot LOLLIES

Want to try a lolly that turns your tongue pink but without all the horrid additives of a shop bought one? Well try my beetroot tongue-tingling recipe.

Blitz a banana (1)
Frozen blackberries (200g)
Small peeled beetroots (2, cooked or raw)
Natural yoghurt (4 tbsp)
Honey (2 tbsp)
Apple juice (50ml) or **water**
in a food processor or blender.

HelPING HAND

HelPING HAND

LOUD

Pour into ice lolly moulds and stick a stick into each lolly. If you don't have an ice lolly mould, you could make miniature lollies using an ice-cube tray and cocktail sticks. You could also save old lolly sticks and yoghurt pots, clean them and use them to make your lollies.

Freeze overnight and enjoy!

makes 2 Lollies

HANDY HACK
If you are having trouble getting your ice-lolly from the mould, then run some warm water over the outside and the lolly will slip out.

The NOT-SO-GreAT POETRY CORNER

BeeTROOT BROWNIES

Beetroot in a cake? Why not, I say! With all this talk of Valentine's Day, why not skip the love hearts and mushiness and make your friends a beetroot brownie for Pal-entine's Day instead. Here's my beety recipe that I bring to the shed for all my fellow GIYers.

makes 12

Chop beetroot (3 medium, peeled and cooked) into chunks.

Lightly steam the beetroot by placing it in a bowl, sprinkling in a little **water** (3–4 tbsp) and microwaving for 10 minutes on a high setting, or until the beetroot is tender when tested with a fork.

Handy Hack
You might want to cover your hands with gloves to prevent them turning red from the beetroot.

Blitz butter (100g)
Vanilla extract (1 tsp)
Milk chocolate or dark chocolate chunks (200g) and the tender beetroot in a food processor. The chocolate and butter will break down in the mixer.

Mix eggs (3) and
Caster sugar (250g, golden or regular) with an electric whisk or by hand if you're up for an arm workout. I like to whisk away all my worries when I have a bad day. Mix this mixture (*say that ten times quickly*) with the other ingredients you blitzed in the food processor.

Sieve cocoa powder (25g) and
Plain flour (100g) and gently fold* your dry ingredients into the rest of the wet mixture and mix it into a nice brownie batter.

*This means use a spatula or wooden spoon to gently add the dry ingredients to the wet mixture. Don't actually try and fold it – that would be tricky and sticky!

Line a small square (20cm) baking tin with baking paper greased with butter and pour in the brownie batter.

Bake in a preheated oven at 180°C for 25 minutes or until the brownies have risen. Leave them to cool.

Cut into squares and enjoy!

MONTY AND THE HORSe POO

Veg plants love poo to help them grow,
So we always add poo before we sow,
Poo from a hen or a cow or a sheep called Saul,
But Poo from horses is the best poo of all.

Because it's important for this veg patch of mine,
I think about poo nearly all of the time,
Mrs Potts says 'Dear Monty, this poo thing is strange'.
I nod, but I'm thinking about the dung I'll arrange.

A trip to a farmer with shovel in hand,
A big pile of horse poo, that will be grand,
But wait, how on earth will I transport this doo-doo?
I forgot the bags, a catastrophic boo-boo!

Straight into the car boot, that is the answer,
The farmer must think I'm a bit of a chancer,
I swear him to secrecy, he smiles and he winks,
And to this day Mrs Potts says, 'This car still stinks!'

Culinary County Lt...

MARCH

March is the first real month of spring for GIYers and the first of three *really* busy months for us here in GIY as we get sowing, in particular our potato planting on St Patrick's Day. Everywhere you look things are starting to grow – little seedlings popping up to say hello *(hurrah!)* and weeds *(booo!)*.

1 It's **springtime**!	2	3 Sing a song in the shower.	4	5 Pick some daffodils.	6	7 Read an Amazing Book Day (and when you're done give it to a pal).
8 Hug your mum, sister, aunt or granny (or all together).	9 Give up something or start something new.	10 Stay up late and stargaze.	11	12 Bring some raw carrot sticks to school in your lunch box.	13	14 Learn a new card game.
15 Ides of March–first day of Roman New Year (beware!)	16	17 *St Patrick's Day!* Prove your Irishness by sowing spuds and dying your hair green.	18 Impress your friends with your green hair!	19	20 Spring Equinox. Day and night are the same length now.	21 Paint some rocks with watercolours.
22	23 Investigate soil with a magnifying glass ...	24 ... but don't fry any ants! What did they ever do to you?	25 Have a meat free day.	26 Have a homework free day.	27 Have a nap.	28 Hold on to plastic bottles to recycle into a watering can (p. 23).
29 Bake some cookies.	30 Share your cookies.	31 Prep your April Fool's Day pranks.	Malaki Hawaiian: *malakee*	Maaliskuu Finnish: *maliskoh*	ມີນາ Lao: *mina*	

AND NOW FOR THE WEATHER

Spring is in the air and the weather warms up a little with average temperatures of 7°C.

But March can still pack a cold surprise. In 2018, Storm Emma collided with the Beast from the East to bring the worst snow seen in Ireland in thirty-six years.

The sea is at its coldest in February and March, so pack away those swimming trunks!

The days are getting longer by about two hours in total over the month.

Amaze your parents by rolling out the phrase: 'There's a grand stretch in the evenings.'

This month to SOW:
- ✓ Potatoes (outdoors)
- ✓ Lettuce
- ✓ Spinach
- ✓ Leeks
- ✓ Coriander (likes to be cosy, so keep indoors)

DON'T FORGET:
- ✓ It's spring, be happy!

This month to HARVEST:
- ✓ Kale
- ✓ Purple sprouting Broccoli

Other jobs:
- ✓ Start nightly slug patrols
- ✓ Keep on top of weeds

March JOBS

If you have a vegetable patch at school or at home, you might see some weeds starting to grow this month. Keep on top of them now before they take over. My favourite tool in the shed is a **hoe**, which I use for weeding. Here's a secret: the best time to weed with a hoe is when there are no weeds! That way you upset the weed seeds just before they germinate and stop them in their tracks.

Hoe

This month I will also sow our potatoes outside in the garden. Keep reading to find out more.

Not you...

In March I will often use a **fork** to turn the soil in my beds lightly. This will get them ready for sowing into the following month.

March is the first month when we really get stuck into seed-sowing. Indoors you can sow lettuce, oriental greens, spinach, celery, celeriac, leeks, broccoli, cauliflower, scallions and kohlrabi.

BIG WORD ALERT

Kohlrabi is a turnip-like veg coming from the German words for cabbage (kohl) and turnip (rabi).

GET CRAFTY in March

Hold on to any used water bottles and upcycle them into watering cans.

HELPING HAND

Get some help to make between five and ten holes in the lid of a 500ml water bottle using a maths compass. (Careful now!) This is tricky work, so get help and take your time.

Fill your bottle with water and watch how the water gently sprinkles out when you hold it upside down. All you have to do now is shake the bottle over your seedlings to hydrate them.

You can even invent your own watering dance moves while you do it. I know I like to!

MAKE A WATER BOTTLE WATERING CAN

The potato we know and love today is believed to have been introduced to Europe in the 1500s by Spanish conquistadors – explorers who travelled the world in search of new lands. I suppose they were a little bit like me only I collect recipes and garden tips. They are said to have brought the potato back from their travels to South America.

Archaeologists believe that the Incas and the Andes mountain people may have fertilised their potato crops with 'guano' (bird and bat droppings) and have found evidence of potato crops at Lake Titicaca dating back to 500 AD.

Potatoes have almost all the nutrients we need to survive, and that's why they became popular among poorer people in Ireland in the past who often lived on just potatoes and milk.

But in the 1840s a plant disease called blight wiped out all the potato crops in many countries of Europe. Named *Phytophophora infestans*, meaning 'vexing plant destroyer', blight is a fungus that spreads in mild and moist climates.

So, you can imagine that the Irish weather was the perfect place for the nasty blight to feast on spud crops. The potatoes failed, and there was a famine in Ireland from 1845 to 1852. Because people depended on potatoes, many starved, and others emigrated to America and Canada on famine ships to escape 'The Great Hunger'.

BIG WORD ALERT

Potatoes were popular in Peru, Chile and Colombia – the word 'potato' comes from the Spanish word *patata*. When potatoes first came to Europe, some scaredy-cats were afraid of the rock-like vegetables and called them 'the devil's apples'. But soon potatoes were being grown in large numbers all over Europe.

In 1995, potato plants were brought onboard the *Columbia* space shuttle and became one of the first foods grown in space.

Royal Fashion Alert! Marie Antoinette loved to wear potato blossoms in her hair, and she made her husband Louis wear them too. Poor Louis.

The SPUD spa

Tired, puffy eyes? No problem! Ditch the cucumber and don the spud, I say.

When my eyes are tired I like to chill a potato in the fridge, slice it thinly and place one slice over each eye.

HELPING HAND

It doesn't work as well with mash!

The cooled spud slices moisturise my eyes! Now switch on some relaxing tunes and your shed becomes your very own spud spa sanctuary.

POTATO PETS

Owning a pet can be a lot of work, but if you've always dreamt of being a pet owner, a spare spud can make the perfect potato pet. I like to use one that has sprouted or is too green to eat. They are the perfect shed companion.

Use pipe cleaners for your pet's ears and tail, cocktail sticks as whiskers, a marker to draw on a mouth and glue-on googly eyes.

You can use scraps of card and whatever other crafty bits you can get your hands on to create your own potato mouse, cat, dog or even dinosaur to keep as a pet on your window sill.

Like my spud spaniel Sammy. I've had him for years ... although he went a bit stinky after a few months. They sprout up so fast!

Sammy

Potatoes can be used to remove rust. If you see some rust on your bicycle, take a raw potato half, dip it in washing up liquid or baking soda and rub it over the rusted part.

POTATO MYTHS AND LEGENDS

ARE POTATOES AND SWEET POTATOES RELATED?
No. Although their names are similar, these two vegetables are not related. A sweet potato is a root vegetable and a potato is a tuber. By the way, a potato is just as healthy as a sweet potato and has fewer food miles.

CAN YOU EAT POTATO SKINS?
Yes, the skin is the best part! If you scrub your spud to remove any dirt and cook through, then there's no reason not to. In fact, most of a potato's goodness is near the skin, especially fibre. But if a potato has sprouted or the skin is green, you shouldn't eat it.

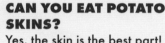

What's wrong with green?

DID SIR WALTER RALEIGH INTRODUCE THE POTATO TO IRELAND?
There are stories of Sir Walter Raleigh bringing potatoes to Ireland from his travels but historians can't agree on this one.

Sir Walter did however plant potatoes on his estate in Cork in the 1500s and is thought to have brought some as a gift to Queen Elizabeth I.

TO LIZ

A rub from a raw potato can bring back the shine to silver items, or you can use the water from boiling potatoes and soak your silverware in it to clean and brighten them. This is because potatoes contain oxalic acid.

MONTY'S KNOW-IT-ALL → STATS ←

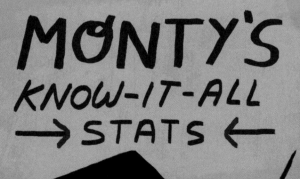

Potatoes are one of the top four most grown crops in the world. The others are rice, corn and wheat.

Potatoes are related to tomatoes and aubergines and are part of the *Solanaceae* family. These are sometimes called the Nightshades, because some like to grow in shady areas and some flower at night.

BIG WORD ALERT

Potatoes are rich in potassium which is good for your blood, bones and muscles. It also helps you go to the loo regularly.

Potatoes are rich in starch like bread, rice, bananas and pasta. They are a healthy carbohydrate. Eating foods like this can make you feel full.

Bees love spuds too. Well, they love pollinating potato plants and are attracted to their flowers.

GROWING POTATOES

We always say in GIY that digging for spuds is like Christmas morning: you never know what you're going to get. Potatoes are an amazing vegetable for growing in a big pot or container – you can even grow them in a big black sack full of soil!

SACK O' SPUDS

	Jan	Feb	Mar	Apr	May	Jun	Jul	Aug	Sep	Oct	Nov	Dec
Sow			✓	✓	✓							
Harvest						✓	✓	✓	✓	✓	✓	

Spud Facts

Potatoes are grown from 'seed potatoes' which are potatoes saved from the previous year. So when you harvest your potatoes you can keep some as the seed to grow next year's potato plants. I like to keep mine under my bed.

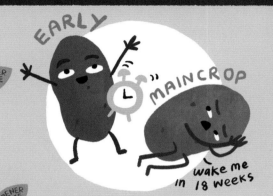

EARLY
MAINCROP
wake me in 18 weeks

GARDENER PHRASE

GARDENER PHRASE

There are two types of potatoes: 'earlies' and 'maincrop'. **Earlies** are sown in March (traditionally St Patrick's Day) and grow quickly. They are ready to harvest in June, about fourteen weeks after sowing. **Maincrop** potatoes are sown in April and stay in the ground longer. They are ready to harvest in September (after about eighteen weeks). Because maincrop potatoes have had time to develop a thick skin, they can be stored over the winter.

Blight, the nemesis of spud-growers everywhere, was responsible for the Great Potato Famine in Ireland (1845–1851). It is an airborne fungus that lands on the leaves of a plant before travelling quickly down to the potatoes in the ground, which then rot. It thrives in the mild, wet, humid conditions of summer. The first signs of blight are dark spots on the leaves. In GIY we use varieties of potatoes that are less likely to get blight like Orla and Sarpo Mira.

CHITTY CHITTY SPUD SPUD

Chitting seed potatoes is where we get the seed potato to sprout to give it a head start before sowing. You can start in February: Lay the seed potatoes in a shallow tray and leave them somewhere bright and cool indoors. By March they will have green sprouts.

SOW

I LOVE MOVING DAY!

How to Sow:
Sow your earlies in mid March, 15cm deep, 25cm apart and 45cm between rows. Sow your maincrop in mid to late April, 15cm deep, 35cm apart and 45cm between rows.

Where to Sow:
I always move my potatoes from one part of the veg garden to another every year because it keeps hungry pests guessing and they like being moved around. This is called 'crop rotation' and it's an important part of organic growing.

GARDENER PHRASE

GROW

Potatoes need 'earthing up'. This is where we draw soil up around the stem (also called a 'haulm') with soil.

Since potatoes grow along the stem, the more of it that is buried beneath the soil, the more spuds you get.

Earthing up is important because potatoes that get too much light near the surface and go green can be toxic to eat.

Cold Out?
Potato plants really don't like frost, so cover young plants with garden fleece if there's any frost forecast.

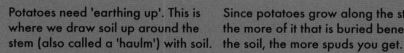

GARDENER PHRASE

Trying *haulming* out loud – it's fun to say when you're having a bad day.

Beware OF the LIGHT

HARVEST

When to Harvest:
I usually harvest my earlies over the summer when I am hungriest and then the maincrop ones in one go in October or November.

I keep them in hessian sacks so they can breathe and don't get stinky. That way I can be sure I have enough roasties on Christmas Day.

Potato plants flower over the summer and it's usually a good sign that they are nearly ready to eat.

BASICS: SOWING SEEDS

As a younger Monty Potts, I sowed seeds for most vegetables in little pots and trays inside the house for planting outside in the soil later. This is a fantastic way to start growing food because instead of sowing them outside in the ground where they have to face all sorts of tests – cold soil, horrible weather, slugs wanting to eat them – they are safe in the warmth of the house.

About three or four weeks after sowing, you plant them out in the soil. They will be happier in their new home. I still sow lots of veg seeds this way, except carrots, potatoes, onions and garlic which are always sown in soil outside or in a large pot or container.

MONTY SHEDDINGTON-POTTS

KEEPING SEEDS

You will probably have loads of seeds left over in the packet after you're finished – these seeds will wait patiently to fulfill their

GIY DESTINY

Have you fulfilled your destiny yet?

Not sure. Have you?

Pop them back in the seed packet and fold the pack carefully. Some veg seeds can be kept for up to three years while others, like parsnip seeds, will only keep for one year.

Store the seeds in a lunch box with a lid and keep it somewhere nice and cool and not too bright. I keep my seed box on the top shelf in the potting shed where Mick can't get his hands on it.

A Seed Sowing MASTERCLASS WITH MONTY

When you start growing, seed sowing can seem a bit of a mystery – sometimes it works, sometimes it doesn't. The main thing you need to know is when to sow the seeds, and how deep. The back of a seed packet is the best instruction manual to find out these things. Then get your seeds, seed trays (the ones with little modules are best) and seed compost and follow these **Easy-Peasy Steps 1-2-3:**

Step 1: Crumble

Time to get your mitts dirty. Tip a little compost out on a table and break it up with your fingers before putting it in the tray. Get rid of all the clumps so the compost is nice and fine. Overfill the tray with compost. Tap the tray against the table a few times to help the compost settle down into it and to remove any air pockets. Top it up with some more compost if you need to – the compost should be level with the top of the tray.

Handy Hack
Use a level piece of wood (like a ruler) to 'slice' any extra compost off the tray to make it level. Not that I would ever be particular about these things ... promise.

Step 2: Sow

The most important thing is to get the depth of the seed right. Sow too deep or too shallow and it might not germinate. Make a little dent in the compost with the top of your finger, pop the seed in and then cover it with compost. Generally you sow one seed per module.

How deep should the seed be?
Well, a good rule of thumb is that it is sowed about twice as deep as its size. Tiny seeds (like lettuce) are usually left on top of the compost*, while larger seeds (like peas) are pushed down into the soil about 1cm.

*Can you remember why? See p. 11.

Step 3: Hydrate

Water it and leave the tray on a sunny windowsill. Usually seeds do best when they have heat and light. It will take between two days and two weeks for the seed to germinate depending on the vegetable. Always keep the compost moist – don't let it dry out. In a few weeks it will be ready to plant out.

STILL OR SPARKLING?

EAT

POTATO HANDY HACK
If you accidentally add too much salt to your soup, just add a few extra potatoes and cook until the salty flavour is reduced.

Give your porridge what I like to call, **The Rhubarb Crumble Treatment**. Add some toasted nuts or granola and some stewed rhubarb and honey for a tangy twist to your breakfast.

WHAT'S IN *March* SEASON

RHUBARB

Make stewed rhubarb:
Get some help to boil chopped rhubarb (750g) in a saucepan with caster sugar (100g – or honey if you prefer), the juice of an orange and 4 tbsp of water for 8–10 minutes until your rhubarb is softened but still has its shape and isn't too mushy.

HelPING HAND

SAVOY CABBAGE
Savoy cabbage is lovely when cooked with just a few tablespoons of water on a pan and tossed about with butter, salt and pepper and, if you're feeling brave, a teaspoon of wholegrain mustard.

SPINACH
Spinach is great in smoothies with banana, berries, apple and yoghurt or milk.

Spinach is also very nice wilted under a poached egg for breakfast.

Spinach is rich in iron and it makes a nice change to lettuce in a sandwich or wrap for lunch.

HERB HERO

ROSEMARY

Did you know?
In the past, rosemary was used to keep moths from eating people's clothes, and in medieval times, it was used to decorate roasted boar head for feasts. In Tudor England, brides wore sprigs of rosemary on their wedding day as a good luck charm. People also thought that keeping a sprig of rosemary under your pillow made you have sweet dreams. Some people still think that the smell of rosemary is calming and can help when you have a headache.

When to sow?
Though you can grow rosemary from seed, it often doesn't work so it's a bit of a waste of time. It's much easier to grow by snipping a cutting off someone else's rosemary plant (ask first!). In May or June, snap a 5–7cm shoot off the plant and take off the leaves from the lower 3–4cm. Put the cutting in a small pot of compost and give it a water.

How to grow?
Keep it nice and warm. A temperature of 17–20°C is needed to help it toroot. After about six or eight weeks, transplant into a bigger pot or plant outside.

Tasty in:

 Lamb

FOCACCIA

ROASTeD VEGeTabLeS

 PIZZA

GNOCCHI

makes enough for 2

People often think that gnocchi is just pasta, but did you know that it's made from potato? Don't gnocchi it until you've tried it. Here is a recipe I picked up from an Italian postman I met in Milano called Giuseppe Postino. He always built up a hunger from gnocchi-ing on doors to give people their post! Gnocchi-gnocchi, who's there? OK, maybe that's enough of that! Time for a gnocchi recipe.

HeLPING HAND

Boil chopped rooster potatoes (1kg) in salted boiling water until they are soft.

Mash the potatoes and make sure the mash is as lump-free as you can get it. If you have a 'potato ricer', then pass the mash through that for extra smoothness.

← RICER

Season with a pinch of **salt and pepper** and transfer to a bowl.

Mix **plain flour** (100g) into the mash. Using a fork, bring the mixture together to make a soft dough. Knead with your hands until you can make the dough into a ball.

Divide the dough into two balls.

Roll each ball into two sausage shaped rolls.

Cut the rolls into 2cm pieces. Using the back of a fork, press each gnocchi gently to give it a nice design and the traditional Italian look.

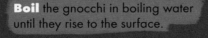

Boil the gnocchi in boiling water until they rise to the surface.

Serve with your favourite **pasta sauce** or **pesto**, some **mozzarella** and a few **basil** leaves.

The NOT-SO-GREAT POETRY CORNER

PATATAS

makes enough for 2

BRAVAS

HeLPING HAND

Patatas Bravas is Spanish for 'spicy potatoes' and this traditional tapas* dish is a recipe for those who are brave enough for the 'bravas'.

*Tapas are small dishes popular in Spain.

Cut potatoes (4 large) into small cubes and dry with kitchen paper.

Spread the cubes evenly across a roasting tin and toss them in **olive oil**, making sure all the potatoes get some olive oil attention.

Season with a pinch of **salt**, **pepper** and some **chilli flakes** if you are feeling brave.

Roast in a hot oven for 45 minutes until the potatoes are golden and crunchy. Shake halfway through the cooking so they are baked evenly.

FOR The Bravas sauce:

Fry an **onion** (1) in olive oil with **Garlic** (a few cloves, chopped) **Paprika** (1 tsp) **Tomato purée** (1 tbsp)

Serve over your roasted spuds and sprinkle with some fresh **parsley**.

THE RISE AND FALL OF SPUDDY O'SHEA

Potato farmers are a particular breed,
Known for being quite competitive indeed.
'Spuddy' O'Shea was a famous spud farmer,
Had the 'gift of the gab', was a bit of a charmer.
'I grow the greatest spuds,' he often boasted,
'All the others are duds, when fried, mashed, or roasted.'

He had won every trophy, at every spud fair,
From Blarney to Boston, Ballybrack to Bel Air.
Constantly bragging, 'My spuds are world famous',
Much to the annoyance of rival farmer Séamus.
There was no farmer on earth that he could not beat
But was he playing fair, or was he a cheat?

At the Festivale de Spud, a scandal was uncovered,
There was cheating afoot, the papers discovered,
Bribing of judges, a word in their ear,
To make sure he took home the trophy each year.
The judges were crooked, giving prizes for cash,
And Spuddy was disqualified for bribing with mash.

APRIL

Don't let April fool you into leaving your umbrella at home. April is famous for its showers! GIYers don't mind that though because Know-It-Alls know that rain is exactly what seedlings need when you are transplanting and planting out this month.

1 April Fool's Day! Play a trick on someone. It's OK to tell white lies today too!

2 Fly a kite.

3 Write a poem. It doesn't have to be good – check out my 'Not-So-Great Poetry Corner'.

4 If it rains today, stick out your tongue and taste it!

5

6 *Invent Your Own Wrap Day.* Bring it to school and let your friends give it marks out of five.

7

8

9

10 Let your sibling have the remote today.

11

12 *Lookalike Day.* Dress like your best friend and confuse everyone.

13 Blast your favourite radio station and get jobs done in the garden.

14 Make some nettle tea. Go to p. 77 to see how it's done.

15

16 Hang kitchen spatulas from the branch of a tree to make unusual wind chimes.

17

18 *High Five Day!* Try and high five as many people as you can today.

19

20 Go on a snail hunt in the dark with a torch.

21

22 *Earth Day.* Give the Earth a hug!

23

24

25 Record the rain on a phone and play it back to yourself in bed as a sleep soundtrack.

26

27

28 Have a kitchen karaoke party and sing along to your favourite songs.

29

30 Organise a mad hair day at school and see who can give themselves the wildest hair style.

ਅਪ੍ਰੈਲ — Punjabi: *apraila*

אפריל — Hebrew: *abrille*

Nisan — Turkish: *nee san*

AND NOW FOR THE WEATHER

In April 1984, a temperature of 25.8°C was recorded in Donegal, while in April 1892 it was –7.7°C in Sligo.

Temperatures continue to rise, but April is always unpredictable.

A severe snowstorm struck Ireland on 1st April 1917. It was snow joke and not an April Fool's prank! There were drifts up to three metres high!

Will it bring sun, rain, wind or snow? Or all four in one day?

GIY LOG BUUK
(NOTHING TO DO WITH LOGS)

This month to **SOW**:
- ✓ BeeTROOT
- ✓ BRUSSELS SPROUTS (IN The Shed)
- ✓ TURNIPS
- ✓ CeLeRY
- ✓ CeLeRIaC
- ✓ COURGeTTe

(OUTSIde) ✓Potatoes
✓OnIons ✓Peas

This month to **HARVeST**:
- ✓ PurPLe sProuTing BroccoLi
- ✓ spring Cabbage
- ✓ Rhubarb

OTher jobs:
- ✓ Keep HoeIng
- ✓ Harden off seedLIngs

Did someone say sprouts?

APRIL JOBS

Slugs become a real nuisance in April; munching on little seedlings before they have had a chance to grow. You can put a ring of crushed eggshells or grit around a seedling to protect it – slugs don't like crawling over rough stuff.

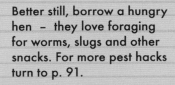

SLUGS Go away (Please)

Better still, borrow a hungry hen – they love foraging for worms, slugs and other snacks. For more pest hacks turn to p. 91.

Because everything starts to grow in April, weeds are growing too. This is a good time to get rid of them when they are nice and little. Get out for some serious hoeing.

Hoe Hoe Hoe

Make an April Fool's scarecrow for your garden to keep birds from pecking your seedlings.

Find an old T-shirt, shirt, hat, leggings or shorts you don't use anymore.

Take two bamboo poles and get a helping hand to join them together in a cross shape with strong twine. Stick your frame into the ground.

Put your old clothes onto the frame and stuff them with straw or garden cuttings. Tie off the ends of the arms and legs with twine to keep all the stuffing in.

Fill an old T-shirt with straw or garden cuttings and tie a knot in it to make a head for the scarecrow. Draw on a face with marker and pop a hat on it.

GET CRAFTY IN APRIL

HERO OF THE MONTH
THE PEA

CHINA

According to archaeologists, the garden pea has been around for thousands of years. They have found peas dating back to 4800 BC in Egyptian tombs in the Nile area.

Pea leaves are considered a delicacy in China.

In the 1860s an Austrian scientist called Gregor Mendel studied the pea pod and mapped how exactly it was formed. This was known as the 'pea genome project', and a lot of modern-day genetics is based on Mendel's pea discoveries.

Pea etiquette rules say that to eat a pea politely, you should squash the pea first with the back of your fork before eating. It also stops them from running around the plate!

The first frozen peas were introduced in 1920.

Thick London fogs in the nineteenth century were often called 'pea soupers' because they were dense and a greenish colour.

'The Princess and the Pea' is a famous story about a prince who seeks to find a true princess. He uses a princess pea test where he places a pea under a pile of mattresses for a princess to sleep on. According to him, only a princess would be able to feel the pea under all the mattresses. The story was first published by Hans Christian Andersen in 1835 but was a folktale among the people for many years before then.

I can't feel a thing!

Well I can!

Originally the word for a single pea was a 'pease', but it got a bit confusing because people thought 'pease' meant more than one pea. At the end of the seventeenth century it was decided to use 'pea' for one pea and 'peas' for more than one pea.

The older form of the word still lives on in a nursery rhyme that has been passed down for centuries:

'Pease-porridge hot, pease-porridge cold,
Pease-porridge in the pot, nine days old.
Some like it hot, some like it cold,
Some like it in the pot, nine days old'.

I'm not sure I'd put peas in my porridge – particularly if they were nine days old!

PEA SACK cornhole

If you have any dried peas that are past their best, don't throw them out. You can use them to make your own cornhole game.

1 Have a look in your recycling for an old cereal box and old scraps of coloured paper, and you'll need to find some old socks – clean ones without holes in them – nobody wants to play a game with stinky socks!

2 Fill the socks with old dried peas and tie a knot to secure them inside.

3 Cut a hole in a cereal box.

HELPING HAND

4 Cut out a triangle on coloured paper and stick it to the cereal box, pointing toward the hole. Time to play!

Rules of cornhole

Each player takes a turn to throw their pea sack and try and get it in the cornhole or as far along the triangle target as possible.

The player who gets their pea sack in the hole or the player who gets their sack closest to the hole along the target, wins the round. I like to play ten rounds.

If you have a bump, a bruise or even a headache, then a cold pea compress can be very soothing.

PEA HACK

Take some peas from your freezer and put them in a small ziplocked bag and pop them into a thin sock.

Press your pea compress on whatever ails you and get well soon.

PEA MYTHS AND LEGENDS

WHAT ARE MUSHY PEAS AND WHY ARE THEY MUSHY?
Mushy peas are dried marrowfat peas that have been soaked overnight in water and baking soda. They are then rinsed, cooked in boiling water and mashed with a little sugar and salt to make them mushy. They are very popular with fish and chips. The term 'mushy pea' was entered into the *Oxford English Dictionary* in 1968.

Kids these days are so... GREEN!

ARE PEAS GREEN OR YELLOW WHEN THEY ARE MATURE?
Peas are yellow when they are mature, but we tend to eat them when they are at their sweetest, which is when they are slightly underripe and green.

IS IT TRUE THAT A PEA IS NOT A VEGETABLE?
Yes! Although we usually think of peas as vegetables, technically they are in their very own food category: legumes.

A true MASTER of DISGUISE

MONTY'S KNOW-IT-ALL → STATS ←

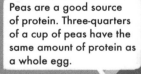

Peas are a good source of protein. Three-quarters of a cup of peas have the same amount of protein as a whole egg.

BIG WORD ALERT

Green peas are part of the legume family *Fabaceae* (along with beans and peanuts), which means they grow pods that hold fleshy seeds. On average, there are eight peas in a pod, but it's always a surprise when you pop the pod to count how many delicious peas are inside.

Peas lose their taste quickly after harvesting them, so you should eat fresh peas as quickly as you can after picking them.

The less water you use when cooking peas, the less vitamin C is lost. Give peas a chance to keep their flavour and don't overcook them! Cook them in just enough water to cover them for about 3 minutes.

GROWING PEAS

Because we usually buy bags of frozen peas, we miss out on one of the perks of growing them yourself – plucking fresh peas from a pea plant to eat.

In GIY, we love a good pea pun – they make us very a-pea.

	Jan	Feb	Mar	Apr	May	Jun	Jul	Aug	Sep	Oct	Nov	Dec
Sow			✓	✓	✓	✓						
Harvest							✓	✓	✓			

It's easy to forget that the pea we eat is actually a seed that could grow into a plant about 4 ft tall which will produce hundreds of other peas. What clever little seeds peas are!

Pea plants are unbelievable – they are called 'nitrogen fixers', which means they take nitrogen from the air and put it in the soil. That means they make the soil better as they grow.

Peas can be grown in lots of different ways. You can grow them in pots or trays to plant out later. Or you can sow them straight in the soil in the garden. You can even cram them into a tray and instead of letting them grow to full size you can eat the tiny little shoots in a salad when they are about 10cm high. Delish!

Oi!

Thanks a mill!

SOW

Where to Sow:
Because they are so easy to grow, I sow my peas outside in the soil, but I wait until it's about 10°C to do so (usually late March).

I make a flat, shallow trench about 15cm wide and 4cm deep and then place the peas 5cm apart in a zig zag along the trench.

↓ 4cm

← 15cm →

Then I cover them over with soil and give them a watering. You could also sow them in a module tray (one pea in each module) and plant them out later. Mick sows his peas in a length of old gutter! Funnily enough, his 'gutter peas' don't sell so well at the market.

GROW

Tips for Growing:
Since peas are hungry plants, the winter before planting, I dig some compost into the soil where I'm going to grow them.

yum!

I also give the soil a few handfuls of organic food like poultry manure pellets (yes, hen poo!) or magic seaweed dust.

Pea plants grow tall so they will need something to climb up, otherwise they will fall over. You can buy pea netting or use twiggy sticks. Pea plants send out tiny little tendrils that are like little hands to grab onto the support.

HARVEST

TADA!

When to Harvest:
Peas are ready to harvest about three to four months after sowing, so we always have a pea party in GIY in

June. Harvesting is easy – we just snap the pod off the plant, and open it for the BIG REVEAL of how many peas are inside. Sometimes the peas don't make it to the kitchen!

I could spend hours in the veg patch watching and wondering; 'How does the pea plant know there's something there to grab on to?'

Peas will need watering outside if there is no rain.

BASICS: PLANTING OUT

When you sow seeds inside the house or in the potting shed, they are usually ready to plant out after about three or four weeks. I like to call this phase the **Silly Gardening Phrase Phase.**

LET'S GET OUT OF HERE!

HARDENING OFF
(Silly Gardening Phrase 1)

GARDENER PHRASE

If you take a little plant that's been grown indoors on a nice sunny windowsill and move it outside all of a sudden, it will get the shock of its life! 'Hardening off' is where we bring the plant outside for a few hours each day to get used to the temperature before bringing it back in again.

If you do this over a week or two then the plant will be ready to move outside for good. At this time of the year, I am carrying trays of seedlings in and out like a yo-yo. Some people like to take their dog for a walk. I like to take my seedlings for a walk.

Time for Walkies!

TRANSPLANTING
(Silly Gardening Phrase 2)

GARDENER PHRASE

If you leave a seedling in a small tray or pot, there comes a time when it will get too big for the pot. It starts to run out of food and its roots curl up around the bottom of the tray (it's called being 'pot bound') because they've nowhere else to go. Time to move it on.

Hmm. I really DO need a bigger place

FOR SALE

Transplanting just means planting the seedling out in the soil or into a bigger pot. You can tell it's ready to move on if you can see the roots coming out the bottom of the tray.

HOW TO 'TRANSPLANT'

1 This bit is delicate. Water the seedlings really well a few hours before transplanting – this will make it easier to remove the seedling from the tray without disturbing the roots.

2 Push the seedling up out of the tray carefully from beneath with your finger. Always hold the seedling by the leaf, not by the stem.

3 Make a hole where you are going to grow the plant (slightly larger than the plant) and then pop the seedling in carefully.

4 Fill in with soil and firm in gently. Water well.

EAT

HERB HERO

MINT

Did you know?
Mint can help settle a funny tummy if you are feeling a bit full or queasy and can help with the hiccups too. Long ago, people used mint leaves on bee stings to soothe them. People also used to grow mint to keep rats away from their crops. They believed that rats were repelled by the strong scent of mint. I've come across many types of mint over the years including spearmint, peppermint, strawberry mint, apple mint, chocolate mint, orange mint and even horsemint, although I've never checked to find out what this actually tasted like – hope it doesn't taste like a horse!

When to sow?
You can grow mint from a cutting, but since it grows so well it's just as easy to buy a little plant and it will grow for years. February or March is the perfect time to plant some mint.

How to grow?
Mint is like a weed; it will grow everywhere if you let it! It's better to grow it in a pot or container which stops it from spreading. Leave 15cm between plants. It likes wet soil, so always keep it watered, particularly if it's growing in a pot.

Tasty in:

WHAT'S IN April SEASON

LEEK

Potato and Leek Soup is a really tasty and filling soup. Cook onion (1), garlic (2 cloves), chopped carrots (2), celery (2 stalks), leeks (3) and potatoes (4) in a large pot with olive oil, then cover with vegetable stock. Simmer on a medium heat for 20 minutes or until the potatoes have softened through.

RHUBARB

Rhubarb is still in season! Stewed rhubarb (see p. 28) topped with granola and yoghurt and a drizzle of honey is a great snack to pop into a jar for lunch.

CABBAGE

Cabbage is still in season! This month, try it in a new way. It can really add to a vegetable soup.

ASPARAGUS

Drizzle a squeeze of lemon and some oil and sprinkle black pepper and salt over the asparagus then cook under a medium hot grill.

Turn the asparagus spears after 3 minutes and make sure each spear gets turned.

IN WATER

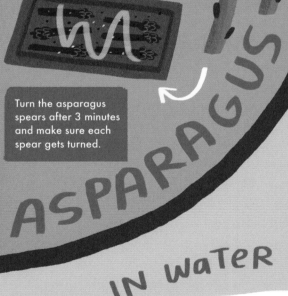

PEAS   Lamb

RASPBERRIES

A POT OF PEA SOUP

Peel and chop shallots (5) garlic (5 cloves).

Dissolve a vegetable stock cube (1) in boiling water (900ml) to make vegetable stock.

Melt butter (2 tbsp) in a pot.

makes enough for 2

Fry the shallots and garlic until their delicious flavour is released (you'll smell the flavour) and they are softened.

Add frozen or fresh peas (800g) to the shallots, garlic and butter and season well with **salt and black pepper**. Stir the peas about and let them start to defrost.

Pour in your vegetable stock, a little at a time, while stirring, then cover your pot with a lid.

Cook your pea soup on a low heat for 10 minutes to allow all the flavours soak in.

Stir in some **fresh cream** (100ml) and take the pot off the heat.

Blitz with a hand blender or in a food processor until smooth and green.

Pour into bowls and enjoy!

HELPING HAND

If you want to go the extra mile, add a sprinkle of chopped mint leaves to impress.

EXTRA MILE

THE NOT-SO-GREAT POETRY CORNER

PEA PESTO

makes 1 jar

Thaw frozen peas (250g) in warm water for a few minutes until they defrost. If you have fresh peas, use them instead.

Blitz shredded mint and basil (handful)
Grated **parmesan** (5 tbsp),
Garlic (2 cloves, peeled),
Olive oil (4 tbsp),
Lemon (a squeeze) and
Salt and pepper (pinch) together with the defrosted peas.

Serve your pea pesto on crunchy toast. Keep in an airtight container in the fridge and eat within three days.

I like to stir my pea pesto into a bowl of pasta with some rocket leaves. It's one of my favourites! Mmmm ... easy, peasy, cheesy pasta!

EXTRA MILE

APRIL MC COOL THE APRIL FOOL

April McCool was 'too cool for school',
Never took advice, and broke every rule.
She lived on the edge, liked to take risks,
Hated vegetables, was addicted to crisps.
She never did warm-ups, never tied her laces,
Even when running in championship races.
She ignored danger warnings and signs saying 'beware',
Never watched where she walked, and never took care.

But one day on a school trip to the city zoo,
April's rule-breaking caused quite a to-do.
'Don't feed the animals', all the zoo signs said,
But April ignored them and fed a hippo French bread.
The hippo was hungry and tugged hard on the stick,
Flinging April right over his head with a flick.
She landed head first in the stinky, hippo pool,
And, covered in dung water, felt a bit of a fool.

MAY

Things are really beginning to bloom this month. I like to ditch my wellies for flip-flops to air my toes in May, but my granny used to say 'never cast a clout 'til May is out' which I think means don't put your warm clothes away until May is over. May **may** be the start of summer or it could still be a bit cold out, so hold onto your vests for now.

1 May Day celebrates the arrival of summer since ancient times.	2 Ooh arrgh! Eat an orange today and keep scurvy at bay, sailors.	3 *Hug a Cat Day!* (Only friendly cats! Watch out for claws!)	4	5 The Mexican festival Cinco de Mayo is today. Tacos, nachos or burritos for dinner?	6	7 *Lost Sock Day.* Organise a lost sock hunt.
8 See if you can spot a swallow. They live in Ireland from April to October before migrating to Africa.	9 Encourage the adults not to cut the grass to grow wild flowers for birds and insects.	10	11	12 Make a daisy chain.	13	14 It's *Chicken Dance Day.* Break out of the coop and bust a move.
15	16 Practise your star jumps and frog jumps.	17	18 Ask your friends to help you collect ice-pop sticks for this month's craft.	19	20 Do some finger painting.	21
22	23 *Lucky Coin Day.* Keep your eyes on the pavement to find a lost coin.	24 Pick wild flowers.	25	26 Make beetroot lollies (p. 21).	27	28
29	30	31 Only one month left until the summer holidays!	**Maggio** Italian: *majo*		**Boaldyn** Manx: *boayldin*	五月 Japanese: *gogatsu*

AND NOW FOR THE WEATHER

It's getting warmer with an average temperature by day of between 13 and 15°C.

The days are lengthening quickly in May. By the end of this month, sunrise will happen just after 5am, and sunset will be at 9:40pm, giving us a whopping sixteen hours of daylight each day!

May can still see cold nights though (not good for tender little seedlings).

In 1979, the Glenties in Donegal recorded a night-time temperature of −5.6°C.

GIT LUUD !!
(NOTHING TO DO WITH LOGS)

This month to SOW:
- ✓ parsnips
- ✓ carrots (outside)

Inside for later transplanting
- ✓ SWEETCORN ↓
- ✓ courgette
- ✓ French beans
- ✓ PUMPKIN
- ✓ cucumber
- ✓ Leeks ✓ celery
- ✓ Beetroot ✓ Turnip
- ✓ Sprouts ✓ squash

This month to HARVEST:
Very Little! →
- ✓ Broad beans
- ✓ Baby beetroot Later in the month

Other jobs:
- ✓ Put up supports for pea plants
- ✓ Cover brassicas (cabbage, kale) with netting to keep the white butterflies away

May is the last of 'Hungry Gap' months

GET CRAFTY IN May

Now that the weather is a little warmer, you might be having more ice pops. If so, then save your lolly sticks and reuse them as markers for what you've sown.

Clean your ice pop stick and allow it to dry.

Spread out some newspaper and paint your sticks different colours.

Lay the sticks out on the newspaper to dry and paint one side at a time.

LEEK!

MINT

When your sticks are dry you can write the name of the plants you are growing on them using white paint or black marker. Put the stick into the ground next to your plant or in its pot to mark what it is.

Always put the date you sowed the seed and the type of veg it is on the stick so you can check later.

MAY JOBS

GARDENER PHRASE

Beat 'The Hungry Gap'! The Hungry Gap was a time of the year when traditionally people struggled to feed themselves, as they had used up last year's food and were still waiting on the new season's crops. April and May are the worst Hungry Gap months as we wait for the first harvests in June. This is why it's good to preserve 'gluts' of vegetables and fruit in the late summer and autumn (by freezing, drying, pickling, making chutneys, etc.) so that they last well into next year.

GARDENER PHRASE

May is a great month for seed-sowing because everything grows quicker than it did earlier in the year. If you didn't get around to sowing seeds yet, this is a great month to catch up. Tomatoes, chillis and aubergine plants that were sown in February or March should be ready to be planted in their final growing place now – either in the greenhouse, polytunnel or into a bigger pot inside.

Make a **May Bush** in your garden. In Ireland, the tradition of making a May bush, and displaying it in a village, farm or garden, was a celebration of the arrival of summer. It was usually a large hawthorn branch (which flowers in May), driven into the ground and decorated with ribbons or streamers. It's tradition to make a wish when you're finished.

I wish I was included in this book!

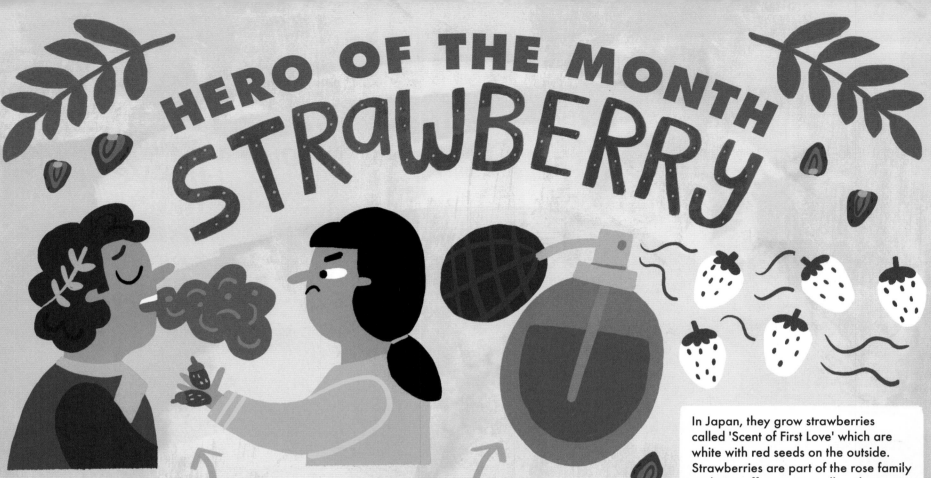

HERO OF THE MONTH
STRAWBERRY

Strawberries were cultivated by Romans as far back as 200 BC, and they believed that they were a cure for bad breath and sore throats.

Strawberries are very fashion-forward as they are the only fruits to wear their seeds on the outside. They have an average of 200 seeds on the outside of each fruit.

In Japan, they grow strawberries called 'Scent of First Love' which are white with red seeds on the outside. Strawberries are part of the rose family and give off a sweet smell as they grow. I can't help sniffing my strawberries as they grow – they smell so good!

In Ancient Greece, the strawberry was a symbol for Venus, the goddess of love.

Ooh! I love the yellow buttons!

Strawberries and cream are famously served every year at the Wimbledon tennis tournament. Two million strawberries on average are served there every year!

Strawberries have always been seen as nature's candy. In the sixteenth and seventeenth century in Britain, strawberries were a luxury food served at special banquets and ceremonies to show off wealth as sweet foods, spices and sugar were considered luxuries.

They were often served at the wedding breakfast of royals as a romantic dish. But is the strawberry actually a berry? (See Strawberry Myths and Legends on p. 41.)

There is a museum devoted to strawberries in Wépion, Belgium, called 'Musée de la fraise'. The village is famous for growing fully ripe, delicious strawberries since the seventeenth century.

X BELGIUM

Freeze-dried strawberries were one of the first foods provided by NASA to feed astronauts. I've always thought that strawberries are so tasty they're out of this world!

BERRY BOUQUET

Instead of giving people bouquets of roses, I like to make bouquets of strawberries – roses and strawberries are cousins after all.

CUT HERE

Get some cake pop sticks or skewers (watch out for pointy tips!) and place a strawberry on top with the leaf pointing down.

With a plastic knife, carve little petals all around the bottom of the strawberry, turning the stick as you go.

Build your petal cuts into the strawberry layer by layer until it looks like a rose.

STRAWBERRY HACK

If you want to remove the centre from a strawberry, here is a handy hack. All you need is a straw to hull the strawberry.

Pierce your strawberry with a straw and push it through to make a tunnel in the centre.

If you like, you can slide the strawberry back onto the straw and use it as a tasty straw decoration when serving drinks at parties.

STRAWBERRY MYTHS AND LEGENDS

ARE STRAWBERRIES SWEETER WHEN THEY ARE WARMER?
Yes! Strawberries served at room temperature taste sweeter than cold strawberries!

DO STRAWBERRIES RIPEN AFTER THEY ARE PICKED?
Nope. Unlike other fruits, strawberries don't continue to ripen after picking.

am I bitter?

ARE STRAWBERRY LEAVES EDIBLE?
Technically yes, but they taste bitter. If you do eat them, make sure they are clean first. A mouthful of bugs is never nice!

IS A STRAWBERRY A TRUE BERRY?
Berries usually have their seeds on the inside, so strawberries are kind of in their own category. The strawberry is called an 'accessory fruit' which means that the fleshy part we eat is actually the stem of the plant.

GARDENER PHRASE

MONTY'S KNOW-IT-ALL → STATS ←

Strawberries are made up of over 90 per cent water.

Strawberries are very high in vitamin C. They have much more vitamin C than grapefruit or blackberries.

BIG WORD ALERT

Strawberries are said to brighten the colour of your teeth because they contain malic acid, a tooth-whitening agent.

But beware! Strawberries also contain natural sugar, so if you do end up using your own mushy strawberry toothpaste to brighten your teeth, you'll need to brush after, or you'll be taking a trip to the dentist for cavities.

BIG WORD ALERT

Strawberries get their bright red colour from anthocyanidin which is like a natural food colouring.

GROWING STRAWBERRIES

They are the great taste of summer, easy to grow and will grow brilliantly in a container or hanging basket.

	Jan	Feb	Mar	Apr	May	Jun	Jul	Aug	Sep	Oct	Nov	Dec
Sow			✓	✓					✓	✓		
Harvest						✓	✓	✓	✓			

First Steps

We start off growing strawberries by buying little plants from a garden centre, but later in the year we can create our own new plants by taking cuttings from the original plants.

GARDENER PHRASE

Running Around

Strawberries send out 'runners' after fruiting in the late summer. If you put a pot of compost under these runners, they will take root. Then snip the runner off the mother plant and, hey presto, you have a brand new strawberry plant that you can plant out next year. Strawberry plants are healthy for about three or four years. After that I replace them with new plants from cuttings.

Straw-berries

I always put some straw on the ground around my strawberry plants – this keeps the fruit nice and clean and also stops weeds from growing.

SOW

Before You Sow:
Strawberry plants are hungry little lads so I always add plenty of well rotted compost to the soil and a handful of poultry manure pellets before planting.

They also like their roots to be dry and deep so I make a little mound of soil and plant in that. Plant them somewhere sunny and sheltered.

They also do really well in pots, growbags or containers, so anyone can grow strawberries. Plant them in September or October somewhere sheltered and sunny.

GROW

Getting Cold?
As the little white flowers develop in May (these flowers will turn into delicious strawberries), they can get damaged by frost so you might need to cover them with garden fleece.

When they are producing fruit from June onwards, it's a good idea to give them a liquid feed (comfrey tea or tomato feed).

Birds love strawberries too – I cover the plants with netting when they are fruiting in the summer to stop them pecking at the fruit.

PECK !OFF!

HARVEST

When to Harvest:
If your plants are healthy you can be eating fresh strawberries for two to three months.

MUNCH away!

Once they are finished, I take off the straw and netting to let birds get in to munch on the pests like slugs.

Let's get out of here!

BASICS: GROWING IN SMALL SPACES

A lot of people avoid growing because they think they don't have the space for it, but Know-It-Alls know that even the smallest space can be your very own GROW HQ.

MONTY SHeddiNGTON-PottS

CONTAINER GROWING BASICS

MONTY'S MIRACLE FOOD

What type of container?
Pretty much any container can be used to grow vegetables, so let your imagination run wild! Pots, troughs, hanging baskets, window boxes, grow bags, wheelbarrows, old watering cans or sinks, wellies or tyres.

What kind of food?
When growing in containers, I make up a mixture of top soil, potting compost and well rotted garden compost or manure. That means there's plenty of food to give the plants a good start.

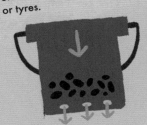

MULCH

What size?
The bigger the container the better! A minimum of 15cm deep is good, but deeper is better, particularly for root vegetables like carrots or deep-rooted plants like tomatoes. Put drainage holes in the base of the container. In deeper containers put in a centimetre layer of small stones to help with drainage.

How much water?
Because the roots can't travel off looking for food and water, container-grown plants usually need extra watering and feeding. You might need to water containers twice a day in very hot weather. Put some bark, straw or well rotted compost on the surface (this is called a 'mulch') to stop the water in the soil from evaporating.

What to grow?
Try any of the following: pumpkins, lettuce, potatoes, carrots, beetroot, courgettes, kale, spring onions, tomatoes, peppers, peas, beans.

THREE SMALL SPACES TO GROW IN

Inside the House
A sunny windowsill is basically like a greenhouse so it's ideal for getting seeds going and growing plants that like heat, like tomatoes, chilli peppers or pea shoots. Most herbs will do well indoors too – try parsley, thyme, coriander, mint, lemon balm, sage and basil. Plant a window box of quick-growing salad leaves (like mizuna, pak choi, rocket or mustard) and keep it inside. Sow every two or three weeks for a continuous supply and to cut down on your shopping list.

On a Balcony
I met a man from Singapore once who grew $700 worth of veg in pots and containers in a very small apartment balcony in just one year. He had a mini greenhouse and stashed pots wherever he could. He used his balcony railing for climbers like cucumbers, tomatoes and climbing beans. If he was living in this part of the world he might need to use netting as a windbreaker because our balconies are a little bit windier.

In a Small Garden
At GROW HQ we have a show garden that's the same size as the average garden. We have three raised beds, a greenhouse, a hen coop and a beehive! There's also a patio and a small lawn but no clothes line or trampoline ... yet.

FIVE WAYS CONTAINER GROWING IS BETTER THAN REGULAR GROWING

No Slugs
Particularly if you live in a tenth floor apartment

No Digging
Keep your back in tip top shape

Handy
Have them right outside the door or inside the house

Mobile
When it gets cold, simply bring containers inside

No Weeding
Well, not much anyway

EAT

STRAWBERRY RULE
Only wash strawberries just before eating them. Strawberries are like little sponges and soak up water. If they get too wet, they will get mushy or mouldy a lot faster.

HERB HERO →

CHIVES

WHAT'S IN May SEASON

CAULIFLOWER

Blitz cooked cauliflower in a food processor to make cauliflower rice or add to a vegetable curry, or try my Curried Cauliflower Wings on p. 12.

RADISH

Radishes are great in salads, even the young leaves! I like to make a radish salsa to eat with fish tacos by chopping some peppers (green and yellow), coriander leaves, radishes, cucumber, shallots, garlic and chilli and dress with lime juice.

CHARD

Use chard in the same ways you'd use kale. You can eat it raw in salads or gently steamed. It also goes great with fish and mashed potatoes.

I like to use mine on pizza with cheese! Keep an eye out for rainbow chard too; it looks great in party salads for summer BBQs.

Did you know?

It's not just the stems of a chive plant that can be eaten; the bulbs beneath the soil are like tiny onions, while the flowers are edible and look amazing in a salad too. Chives are in the same family as onions and garlic, and they have a similar taste. They are also related to the lily flower but smell a lot stronger! A bunch of chives could be mistaken for a bunch of grass. You can play a trick on your friends by eating chives and telling them you are eating grass. People used to hang dried bunches of chives in their homes to ward off evil spirits. I know that vampires don't like garlic so I guess evil spirits mustn't like chives!

When to sow?

Growing chives from seed is easy. Sow the seeds in a module tray or pot filled with potting compost in March or April. Keep the compost moist. Transplant into bigger pots (with fresh compost) or into the ground outside about a month later, leaving 10cm between plants. Chives grow well in pots or containers, just make sure the compost in the pot never dries out.

How to grow?

Don't harvest at all in the first year until July, to give the plant a chance to grow. When you harvest, use a scissors to snip; leaving 5cm of stem behind. You can usually harvest the leaves many times during the season. Chives are perennial so they grow back year on year. They will do well in most soils in full sun or some shade.

SOUP GARNISH ↘

POTATO

Tasty in:

SALAD ↗

EGGS ↖

CREAM Cheese

FROZEN yoghurt STRAWBERRIES

Chocolate covered strawberries are a great party treat and are easily made by dipping strawberries in melted chocolate (white, milk or dark) but, as the weather heats up in May, I find I'm always tempted by the sound of the ice-cream van but never catch up with it in time to beat the queues so I like to keep these frozen yoghurt treats in the freezer instead. It saves me chasing the ice-cream man.

Wash fresh strawberries (20) but leave the stems on (you'll need something to grab on to when you are dipping the strawberries in yoghurt, and it makes eating them easier too).

HeLPING HAND

Mix thick natural yoghurt (150ml) with Vanilla essence (1 tsp) and Honey (2 tbsp)

or you can use a vanilla yoghurt if you like.

NATURAL YOGHURT

Place a wire cooling rack (the type used for baking) over a tray to stop any dripping yoghurt sticking to your freezer later.

RACK   TRAY

Dip the strawberries in yoghurt and place on the wire rack with the stems down and fruit up.

Freeze for two hours.

makes 20

Keep the rest of your yoghurt mixture covered and in the fridge for further dipping later.

Remove the strawberries from the freezer and dip them in yoghurt again. Put them back on the rack.

Freeze for another two hours or until you are ready to serve them.

The NOT-SO-GREAT POETRY CORNER

Oven-dried STRAWBERRIES

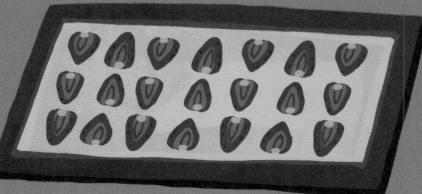

Make your own candy from **Nature's Candy** by drying out some fresh strawberries.

HeLPING HAND

Preheat your oven to 100°C.

Slice fresh strawberries (as many as you like, but make sure you have enough trays to roast them all).

Line a tray with baking paper.

Place the strawberry slices on the tray, making sure they are evenly spaced.

Roast the strawberries in the oven for two hours at 100°C.

Remove the strawberries from the oven after two hours and turn them with a fork. They'll be quite dry by now, but now the other side needs to dry out.

Roast in the oven for another hour at 100°C.

Remove from the oven and allow to cool.

Store in an airtight container.

Serve on breakfast cereal, desserts, or just eat as a treat.

A SLUG'S LIFE

Shane is a slug who lives in the ground
He creeps around without making a sound
His slime is green, his moustache is pink
If you see him around, give him a wink

He likes to hang out in all the cool places
Under stones or planks, he's loving dark spaces
He stays hidden all day, not a fan of sun
It's only at night that he comes out for fun

He devours a leaf in three seconds flat
Be it spinach, lettuce or anything like that.
A wave of destruction he leaves in his wake
He thinks about chard like you think about cake.

He hates crawling over a broken eggshell
It hurts, it scratches and boy does it smell
Coffee grinds are also his least favourite thing
They don't wake him up, they just really sting.

His two greatest fears are slug pellets and salt
He's known for being slimy but that's not his fault
He's nervous of birds while out eating kale
He'd love to have a shell and be more like a snail.

JUNE

School's out and the sun's out! If you've been a busy sower, then this month you'll start to see that you are now a full blooming grower! Longer days mean you'll have even more time to spend on your plot in the evenings. If you're planning to head off on your holidays, ask a green-fingered neighbour to keep an eye on your plot or pots for you.

1 Practise flipping a coin. Pick a side: heads or tails?

2 Start collecting plastic bottles and garden clippings for a bug hotel (p. 47).

3 Show your friends your new coin flip trick.

4 Try a new cheese today! There are thousands to choose from.

5

6

7

8 Record the time of the sunset.

9

10

11 Try juggling two apples.

12 Get your swimming trunks ready.

13

14

15 Step up your juggling practice and add a third apple to your routine.

16 *Bloomsday!* We celebrate the great Irish writer James Joyce and his famous book *Ulysses* today. Carry a potato in your pocket like Bloom and try some Gorgonzola. **17**

18

19 Try a yoga 'warrior pose' in your garden to stretch and feel good.

20

21 Notice how long the summer days are and how long the sun stays in the sky today.

22

23

24 Pick some gooseberries.

25

26

27 Holidays are coming ...

28 Holidays are coming ...

29 Any day now ...

30 School's out for summer!

Június Hungarian: *yuneeoos*

जून Hindi: *june*

Pipiri Maori: *pipiri*

AND NOW FOR THE WEATHER

The longest day of the year (the Summer Solstice) is on 21st June, and after that date the days will start to get shorter.

Watching the weather was important in setting the date for the D-Day landings in the Second World War. In June 1944, forecasters were watching the wind, sea conditions and cloud cover. The landings were planned for 5th June but had to be postponed until 6th June because of bad weather.

Ireland's highest ever temperature of 33.3°C was recorded in Kilkenny on 26th June 1887.

Average sea temperatures this month are a balmy 12.3°C

GIY LOG BOOK
(NOTHING TO DO WITH LOGS)

This month to SOW:
- ✓ CARROTS
- ✓ Kale
- ✓ PURPLE Sprouting Broccoli

Don't FORGET:
- ✓ Put supports in place for runner beans, peas + broad beans

This month to HARVEST:
- ✓ GARLIC → around longest day
- ✓ Broad Beans
- ✓ Peas
- ✓ New Potatoes

Other jobs:
- ✓ Net soft fruits to keep the birds away

JUNE JOBS

If you have a greenhouse or polytunnel in the garden, you will need to water the plants daily. If the weather is dry, plants outside in the ground and in pots will also need watering.

Earthing up potato plants stops the spuds from going green under the soil and helps you to get even more spuds. 'Earthing up' means gathering soil around the stem of the plant.

GARDENER PHRASE

June is a great month for planting out seedlings that were started off in pots or trays. Plant out leeks, cabbage, pumpkins, courgettes, squashes, runner beans, celeriac, celery and more.

Taxi! I'm out of here

Get Crafty in June

MAKE A BUG POD!

Get some help to cut two cylindrical tubes from a large plastic bottle.

Gather twigs, leaves, grass and twigs from your garden or from a nature walk.

Stuff the tubes with the garden cuttings you've collected. Bugs will be able to crawl in from either side.

You can tie garden twine around the cylinder and hang one of your bug pods off a tree branch. You can also leave it in a corner of your garden or balcony – anywhere you think there might be insects who'd like to try out your cosy pod.

MAKE A BUG LOG CABIN!

If you find a nice block of wood, then ask a helping hand to drill some holes in it. Then you can stuff it with twigs and garden cuttings, or leave it empty for insects to crawl into.

HERO OF THE MONTH
COURGETTE

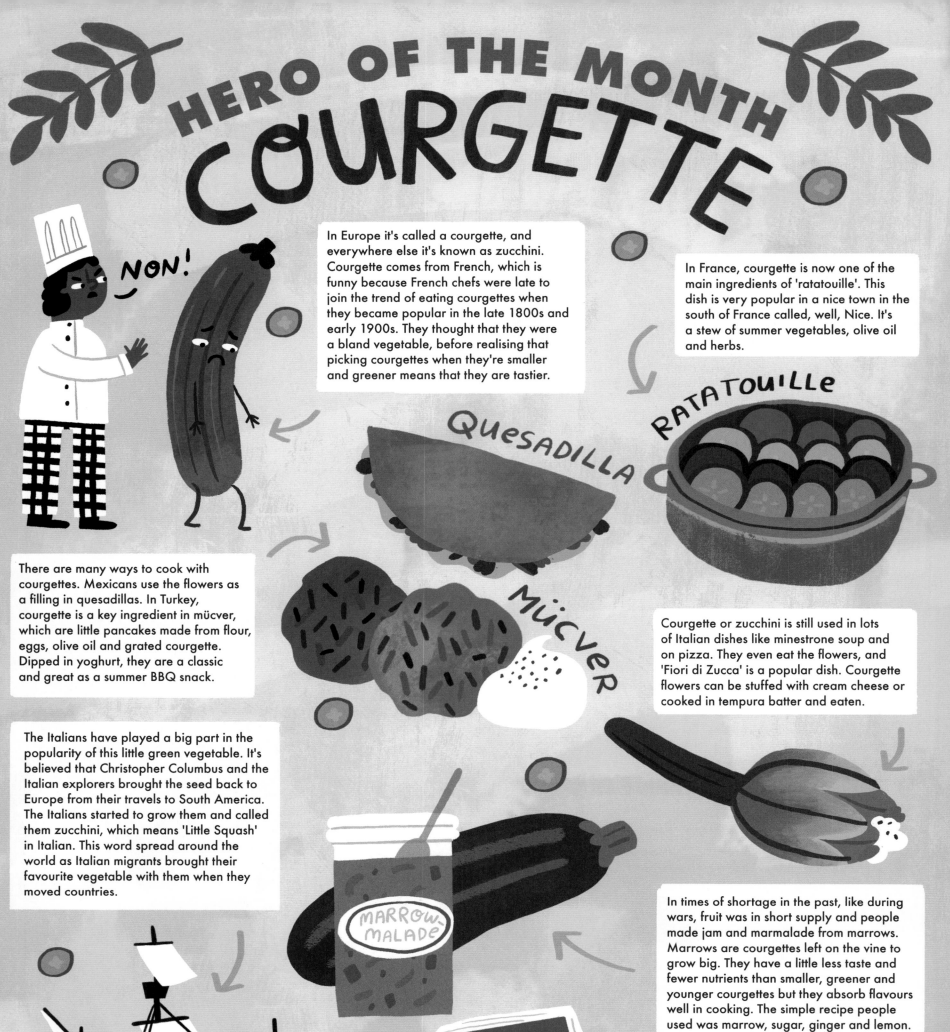

NON!

In Europe it's called a courgette, and everywhere else it's known as zucchini. Courgette comes from French, which is funny because French chefs were late to join the trend of eating courgettes when they became popular in the late 1800s and early 1900s. They thought that they were a bland vegetable, before realising that picking courgettes when they're smaller and greener means that they are tastier.

In France, courgette is now one of the main ingredients of 'ratatouille'. This dish is very popular in a nice town in the south of France called, well, Nice. It's a stew of summer vegetables, olive oil and herbs.

QUESADILLA

RATATOUILLE

There are many ways to cook with courgettes. Mexicans use the flowers as a filling in quesadillas. In Turkey, courgette is a key ingredient in mücver, which are little pancakes made from flour, eggs, olive oil and grated courgette. Dipped in yoghurt, they are a classic and great as a summer BBQ snack.

MÜCVER

Courgette or zucchini is still used in lots of Italian dishes like minestrone soup and on pizza. They even eat the flowers, and 'Fiori di Zucca' is a popular dish. Courgette flowers can be stuffed with cream cheese or cooked in tempura batter and eaten.

The Italians have played a big part in the popularity of this little green vegetable. It's believed that Christopher Columbus and the Italian explorers brought the seed back to Europe from their travels to South America. The Italians started to grow them and called them zucchini, which means 'Little Squash' in Italian. This word spread around the world as Italian migrants brought their favourite vegetable with them when they moved countries.

MARROW-MALADE

In times of shortage in the past, like during wars, fruit was in short supply and people made jam and marmalade from marrows. Marrows are courgettes left on the vine to grow big. They have a little less taste and fewer nutrients than smaller, greener and younger courgettes but they absorb flavours well in cooking. The simple recipe people used was marrow, sugar, ginger and lemon.

Diary of a Courgette

HMS ZUCCHINI

In 2012, astronaut Don Pettit, nicknamed 'Gardener', decided to try and grow a courgette from seed in a small plastic bag in space. The plant even had its own diary which told the story of its journey from seed to plant. If you plant courgettes, you could keep a courgette diary or write the story of what happens. My first courgette book was called *The Adventures of Babette the Courgette*.

Some historians have reported that George Washington and Thomas Jefferson, both presidents of the United States, were big zucchini enthusiasts and loved growing them.

Courgetti Spaghetti

If you have a fancy gadget called a 'spiraliser' at home, you can make spiral noodles that you can cook and eat in the same way as spaghetti.

If you don't have that fancy gizmo, you can do what I do which is to use an everyday vegetable peeler to peel thin strips of courgette to make my courgetti spaghetti.

I cook it in a shallow pan with olive oil and chopped garlic for 3–4 minutes and then I serve it with chopped basil and grated cheese. I'm making myself peckish at the thought of it!

LIGHTEN UP

If you have a courgette which has grown into a marrow that you aren't going to eat, you can carve it like a pumpkin!

You can put a night light inside as a lantern for summer garden parties or BBQs.

Don't wash your courgettes before storing in the fridge. Courgettes are like sponges and doing this can make your courgettes get soggy.

COURGETTE MYTHS AND LEGENDS

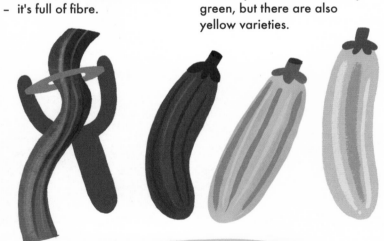

CAN YOU EAT COURGETTE RAW?
Yes. You can also eat the skin – it's full of fibre.

ARE COURGETTES ALWAYS GREEN?
No. They are most commonly green, but there are also yellow varieties.

ARE BIGGER AND LIGHTER COLOURED COURGETTES TASTIER?
No, it's the smaller, darker and younger courgettes that have the most nutrients and tend to be tastier. The bigger they get, the blander the taste, so we harvest when they are smaller and tastier.

IS A COURGETTE A FRUIT?
Know-It-Alls like myself like to know that, botanically speaking, courgettes can be called a fruit because they have seeds and come from the flower of the plant. But we call courgettes a vegetable and treat them as one for growing and cooking.

BUT DON'T PUT ME IN A FRUIT SALAD!

MONTY'S KNOW-IT-ALL → STATS ←

You can eat the skin and the flower of a courgette.

GARDENER PHRASE

Courgette is an 'annual' plant, which means that it completes its life cycle in one year.

They are a very fast-growing vegetable, especially in summer. You won't believe your eyes when you see how quickly you have courgettes to harvest!

Courgettes are related to pumpkins, melons and cucumbers.

Courgettes have more potassium in them than a banana, they are low in sodium and are good for blood pressure and your heart.

GROWING COURGETTES

Courgettes are easy to grow, and in one season you can get up to forty courgettes from one tiny little seed! Your only problem will be working out what to do with all those courgettes. Courgette cake anyone?

	Jan	Feb	Mar	Apr	May	Jun	Jul	Aug	Sep	Oct	Nov	Dec
Sow				✓	✓	✓						
Harvest							✓	✓	✓	✓		

Courgette plants produce so many courgettes, I've been known to wander the neighbourhood with bags of them giving them away for free.

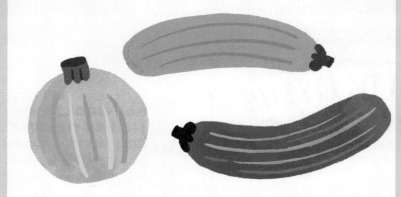

You can grow courgettes of all different shapes, sizes and colours. As well as the standard green courgette, I love to grow a round yellow one that looks more like a melon.

When a courgette gets really big it has basically turned into a marrow.

my, how you've grown!

SOW

When to Sow:
Sow courgettes between April and June. Fill a small pot with compost and sow a seed 1.5cm deep.

Where to Sow:
Keep the pot somewhere warm and sunny (20°C is ideal) and make sure the compost is moist while you are waiting for it to germinate.

GROW

Where to Grow:
In late June, plant it out in the garden or into a much bigger pot with fresh potting compost.

How to Grow:
If you are growing in a container, it will need to be 40–50cm deep. Protect from cold nights with garden fleece if needed.

When planting, keep courgette plants (if you have more than one) 60cm apart and dig in plenty of well rotted compost. Give it a liquid organic feed (like comfrey tea) every two or three weeks. Water well in dry weather.

60cm

40cm
-50cm

HARVEST

When to Harvest:
Try to harvest them when the courgettes are about 20cm long – they taste best when they are nice and small.

You can store courgettes in a cool room or shed for three or four weeks. The more you pick, the more courgettes will grow!

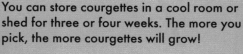

BASICS: POLLINATORS

With the buzzing and the stinging, we might find insects like bees to be a little annoying, maybe even a little scary. But did you know that insects are really important to human beings and to our planet because they help us to grow the food we need to be healthy and happy? Of the 100 crops that provide most of our food around the world, seventy-one of them are pollinated by insects.

Because we are building more and more cities, and because of the way we produce food, insects are having a really tough time surviving on our planet. Every year there are less and less of them, and some are at risk of becoming extinct. This is very bad news indeed ... remember the dinosaurs?

MONTY
SHeddiNGTON-
POttS

The Basics of Pollination

GARDENER PHRASE

POLLEN

STAMEN

'Pollination' happens when pollen, a powder inside a plant's flower, gets moved to another plant so that the plant can start to make seeds which will grow into new plants. Without pollination, plants can't make new plants, so it's pretty important. Sometimes pollen is blown by the wind from one plant to another, but mostly insects do this important work.

Insects visit flowers to get nectar to eat and to collect pollen to feed their babies. Almost by accident, they move pollen from one plant to another. They are like a pizza delivery guy who doesn't know he's delivering pizza. When you see insects like bees buzzing around a flower, you know they are also doing a pollen delivery job.

Thanks!

In Ireland our main pollinators are bees, hoverflies, wasps and butterflies. Believe it or not, queen bees have to visit around 6,000 flowers a day to get enough to eat!

A lot of the veg and fruit we eat (like apples, strawberries, tomatoes, cucumbers, peas, blackberries, pumpkins and beans) need insects to pollinate them. Really, insects are the most important part of the GIY family! Apart from the plants we eat, there are over 2,000 trees and flowers that need insects to pollinate them.

This is not the end of the story. A lot of our animals and birds also rely on insects and bees. This is because they eat the seeds and fruits which have grown thanks to pollination.

TOP 5 TIPS
TO HELP POLLINATORS

The good news is that we can help pollinators by making some changes in our gardens and at school to give insects a place to live and lots of food to eat.

HOTEL

①

Let the grass grow. The grass in our garden looks lovely when it's cut, but if we let it grow we create a habitat for insects to thrive. It lets the wildflowers like dandelion and clover grow, which is great food for insects.

②

Plant wild flowers and shrubs. Shrubs that flower in spring, like willow and hazel, are brilliant for hungry bees just coming out of hibernation. Bees hibernate during the winter months which is why we don't

③

Grow fruit and veg in your garden. Plants like courgettes, strawberries and apples provide food for insects in late spring and summer.

④

Don't use any chemical sprays in your garden. These make insects sick.

⑤

Make a bee hotel. See p. 47 for instructions.

EAT

COURGETTE RULE

Courgettes have lots of water in them, so if you want to chop your courgettes in advance of cooking and you don't want your courgette getting soggy, sprinkle with a bit of salt and let it sit until you are ready to cook it.

I bake 400g gooseberries sprinkled with golden caster sugar on a baking sheet at 180°C for 35 minutes. Then I squish them with a fork in a bowl to release their sweetness and cool. I use my mush on porridge and on top of cheddar cheese on crackers.

HERB HERO

BASIL

Did you know?

The name Basil comes from the Latin for 'royal plant'. There are over a hundred different types of basil; my favourite is purple basil. The Ancient Egyptians used basil to embalm their mummies. Basil tea is said to be good if you're feeling a bit too full after eating. You can make basil tea by popping some leaves in hot water for 3 minutes to steep.

When to sow?

Basil is an annual herb which means we sow it every year from seed. It likes a Mediterranean climate (don't we all) so either grow it indoors in a pot, or in a glasshouse or polytunnel. I sow seeds anytime from April to June in a module tray. It will germinate in about two weeks. When it's about 7–10cm high, transplant into a larger pot or the ground.

How to grow?

When a basil plant has reached about 25cm high, cut off the growing tip of the plant with a scissors. This encourages the plant to get bushy rather than tall and straggly!

WHAT'S IN June SEASON

GOOSEBERRIES

Gooseberries are an easy to grow fruit and can be used to make tasty jams. I like to make Baked Gooseberry Mush with mine.

SPRING ONIONS

Spring onions are great in egg fried rice, stir-fries, toasted cheese sandwiches, omelettes and salads. I like to eat them raw as a little snack, but I always eat a sprig of parsley afterwards to keep my spring onion breath under control.

NEW POTATOES

Let the spuds do the talking. Boil them, roast them, mash them, bake them. I eat mine jackets and all (but do make sure to clean them first).

SPINACH

Spinach is great in salads, wraps, curries, with fish or simply steamed with a little butter, salt and pepper alongside some tasty boiled new potatoes.

One of the most common questions I get asked in GIY is why the basil plants that people buy in supermarkets die when you get them home. Usually the reason is that there is no food left in the pot for the plant. If you pot the plant up in a new, bigger pot with fresh potting compost when you get it home it should last longer!

Tasty in:

pesto sauce

Tomato and mozzarella

Pasta

Pizza

HALLOUMI, COURGETTE & VEGETABLE SHISH KEBABS

If you want to remember how to say halloumi, you can just think of my favourite cheesy joke:

What did the salty cheese say to himself in the mirror?
Halloo-Me!

makes 2 kebabs

This recipe uses one of my favourite types of cheese. It's a salty cheese that makes a kind of squeaky sound sometimes when you eat it. I like to grill my halloumi on the BBQ in summer and it goes well with summer vegetables for Shish Kebabs *(try to say that ten times fast!)*.

HELPING HAND

Chop a courgette (1)
Red onion (1)
and a small block of **halloumi** into large chunks.

Thread the vegetables and halloumi chunks onto wooden kebab skewers with whole **cherry tomatoes** and **basil leaves**.

Mix olive oil (3 tbsp),
Balsamic vinegar (1 tbsp) and
Lemon juice (1 lemon) into a dressing.

Drizzle the dressing over the kebab skewers and turn the skewers so all of the vegetables and cheese are covered.

Season the skewers with **salt and pepper** and leave aside to soak in the flavours of the dressing and seasoning.

Grill on a BBQ or under a grill for 8 minutes, turning regularly to make sure all sides of the kebab are cooked.

Serve with a pinch of **chopped basil**.

THE NOT-SO-GREAT POETRY CORNER

COURGETTE CANOES

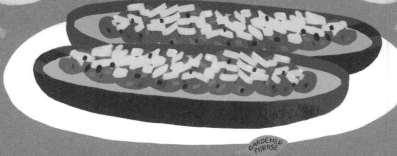

GARDENER PHRASE

If you end up with a courgette glut like I often do in the summer months, invite some GIYers around for tea and treat them to a toastie with a difference. Why make a toastie on a baguette when you can make one with a courgette?

HELPING HAND

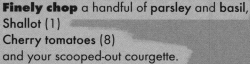

Slice courgettes (3) in half lengthways.

Scoop out a little of the centre of the courgette with a spoon to make space for your filling. Set aside for now.

Grate cheddar cheese (200g) and Crusty bread (100g) to make breadcrumbs (or you can use dried breadcrumbs).

Finely chop a handful of **parsley** and **basil**,
Shallot (1)
Cherry tomatoes (8)
and your scooped-out courgette.

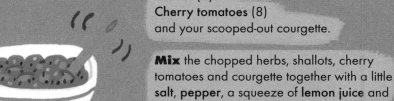

Mix the chopped herbs, shallots, cherry tomatoes and courgette together with a little **salt**, **pepper**, a squeeze of **lemon juice** and a drizzle of **olive oil**.

Fill the courgette canoe with your herby mixture and top with grated cheese and breadcrumbs.

Bake the canoes on a baking tray for 30 minutes at 180°C. Eat and enjoy!

makes 6 canoes

THAT'S SHOW BEES-NIS!

Bernardo de Bumble, the celebrity bee,
Got the starring role in every B movie.

He was a pretty big deal on the pollination scene,
Went to the best parties, was friends with the Queen.

He spent his days chilling, sipping sweet nectar ice tea,
And avoiding getting snapped by bee paparazzi.

He dined at all the best flowers, always caused a buzz
'Cos when he wriggled his bum, pollen stuck to his fuzz.

He had a beehive mansion, and made lots of sweet honey,
The drones laughed at his jokes, even ones that weren't funny.

But the fame got to Bernardo, he stuck up his nose,
Refused to sign autographs or pose for fan photos.

Bernardo didn't care, 'I'm rich and I'm famous,
If bees don't like me, whatever, I'm blameless.'

When he arrived at the Bee Oscars, bees started to boo
Bernardo ignored it, went to fix his hair in the loo.

With his speech in his pocket he was dead sure he'd win,
But a ladybird scooped the prize, oh what a sting!

JULY

Long days of summer means there's lots of time to harvest all your delicious crops and, with sunset that bit later, you'll still have time to BBQ late into the evening and have trampoline parties. Break out the garden hose to keep those veggies alive, but follow our watering tips on p. 59 and be more water conscious.

1 Canada Day. Have some maple syrup on your porridge or on pancakes.	**2**	**3** Eat Beans Day! On toast, in a chilli or on their own. Have a bean bonanza!	**4** Independence Day in the USA. Have a peanut butter and jam sandwich to celebrate like an American.	**5**	**6**	**7**
8	**9**	**10**	**11**	**12** Notice the colour of your friends' eyes.	**13**	**14** Bastille Day in France. Have something French today – even if it's just a baguette.
15 Cow Appreciation Day. If you see one, thank it for making milk for us!	**16** Raspberry Day. Blow a raspberry or eat some on your cereal to celebrate this tasty berry.	**17**	**18**	**19**	**20**	**21**
22	**23**	**24**	**25** Collect used boxes and containers for building impressive sandcastles with!	**26**	**27** Have a sandcastle building competition!	**28**
29	**30**	**31**	Юли Bulgarian: yooli	Julho Portuguese: joolioh	Lulju Maltese: loolyu	

AND NOW FOR THE WEATHER

Average temperatures by day in July are 16°C.

However, in July 1962 in Co. Offaly, the temperature dropped to -3.3°C at night ... brrrr!

Get up early! Sunrise in July is around 5am, and the daylight lasts for nearly seventeen hours.

It can be up to 40°C in a polytunnel or greenhouse in the summer months.

GIY LOG BOOK
(NOTHING TO DO WITH LOGS)

This month to SOW:
- ✓ White Turnip
- ✓ Radish
- ✓ Dwarf French Beans
- ✓ Salad Leaves

This month to HARVEST: EVERYTHING

Don't Forget:
- ✓ Keep Watering
- ✓ 'Earthing up' Leeks will help to make the white part longer

Other jobs:
- ✓ Pinch out tomato side-shoots (p.58)

GET CRAFTY IN JULY

MAKE A MINIATURE WATER BUTT!

Non-Know-It-Alls often giggle when I tell them about my water butt. So rude! Don't they know there are different kinds of butts? Building a miniature water butt is a great way to collect and reuse rainwater to water your plants.

Clean a plastic milk jug and screw the lid on tightly.

HELPING HAND

Cut the bottom off the jug. Turn the bottomless milk jug upside down.

Punch a hole in the plastic on two sides. Loop some garden twine through the hole to hang your new mini water butt somewhere in your garden where it will collect water when it rains.

When your mini water butt is full, you can unscrew the cap so water flows into your watering can and water your plants. Why not record how long it takes to fill? In our climate, probably not very long!

JULY JOBS

I think July is probably my favourite month in the veg patch. A lot of the hard work of the growing year is now done, and we're starting to get lots of lovely food to eat! This month I'm harvesting French beans, runner beans, broad beans, peas, tomatoes, cucumbers, courgettes, beetroot, potatoes, broccoli, cauliflower, cabbage, spinach, carrots, turnips, shallots, garlic, radish, spring onions, salad crops, strawberries and raspberries. Phew! Also I'll be having lots of BBQs to use up all those lovely vegetables.

At this time of the year some veggies (like new potatoes) might be finished, so you can clear the bed they grew in and get it ready to sow something else. This means I get the best use out of the ground.

All yours!

We're not done sowing either! Continue to sow Swiss chard, lettuce, rocket, salad onions, radishes, turnips, peas, French beans (dwarf) and carrots. I like the carrot variety Amsterdam Forcing because you can sow it late in the summer.

Sow me too!

HERO OF THE MONTH
TOMATO

Tomatoes have been grown for thousands of years. The Aztecs grew them in Peru as long ago as 700AD and called them *Xitomatl* which means 'plump thing with a belly button'. The Spanish conquistadors brought tomato seeds back to Europe from their travels to South America in the 1500s.

The world's biggest food fight happens every August in Valencia in Spain during the *La Tomatina* festival. Every year thousands of people come to celebrate tomato season and throw tomatoes at each other. I do hope they only throw the rotten ones. It would be a shame to waste a good tomato.

The Germans originally called tomatoes 'wolf peaches', the French called them 'love apples', and the Italians called them 'golden apples'. It's thought that the first tomatoes grown in Europe may have been yellow.

In the seventeenth and eighteenth centuries, tomatoes were often used as table decorations for special occasions.

There's a story that when the famous band The Beatles wrote their song, 'With a Little Help from My Friends', the first line was originally:

'What would you think if I sang out of tune? Would you throw ripe tomatoes at me?'

But drummer Ringo Starr was worried that fans at their concerts might actually throw tomatoes at them during that song! Beatles fans often caused a frenzy at shows – they called it Beatlemania. The band decided it might be best to change the line to avoid Beatlemania turning into Tomatomania.

In 1984, millions of tomato seeds were sent into space! They circled around the Earth aboard a satellite for six years before they were brought back to Earth and given to millions of schools around the world to plant. Even though the tomato seeds orbited the Earth for six years before being planted, nobody reported any difference between the space seedlings and ordinary earthling tomatoes.

TOMATO TULIPS

Cut an X into a cherry tomato, being careful not to cut through to the bottom.

Gently pull the X you've cut apart with your fingers to make the tomato tulip.

Fill the centre of the tomato with a teaspoonful of hummus or cream cheese.

If you want to go the extra mile, pierce the bottom of the tomato by using a cocktail stick. Now it looks just like the stem of your tulip.

HELPING HAND

EXTRA MILE

MINI Caprese HEARTS

Caprese salad is very popular in Italy. It's a combination of mozzarella, basil and tomatoes. To make a traditional Caprese salad, see the Eat section of this chapter, but in the meantime, why not impress your pals with mini Caprese hearts for a summer party?

HELPING HAND

Cut the top off a cherry tomato at a slight angle.

Place the bigger piece you are left with flat side down and cut in half.

Place the two halves, flat side down, together and make a heart shape with them.

Use a cocktail stick to join them together.

You can cut a little triangle of mozzarella to thread onto one side of the cocktail stick and thread a leaf of basil onto the other side to look like an arrow.

TOMATO MYTHS AND LEGENDS

DEADLY TOMATOES

There was a time in history when people in America thought tomatoes could kill you. This ended in 1830, when a man called Colonel Robert Johnson shocked crowds by eating a bag of them and surviving in Salem, New York. Everyone expected him to die after eating so many tomatoes, but he survived and the myth that they were poisonous was finally put to bed.

DANGER KILLER

ATTACK OF THE CATERPILLARS

Tomatoes might look like friendly fruit, but don't be fooled: they can stand up for themselves when under attack. When caterpillars try to eat them, tomatoes can produce chemicals that make their leaves taste terrible to the caterpillar while at the same time attracting wasps – the caterpillar's mortal enemy.

This tastes off!

Heh heh

MONTY'S KNOW-IT-ALL → STATS ←

When tomatoes are harvested, they continue to gain weight as they continue ripening.

Tomatoes are the fruit of the tomato plant and so have seeds. Tomato seeds aren't easily digested by our bodies so they look the same way coming out of our bodies as they did when they went in! Hens can't digest them either. How do I know? When I feed my hens tomato scraps, I see little tomato seedlings growing where the hens do their dirty doo-doos!

Tomatoes belong to the nightshade family, a name given to plants that people believed grew at night or in shaded areas. We know now that tomatoes grow well in sun but lose their vitamin C very quickly if stored in direct sunlight after harvesting.

Tomatoes lose their flavour if you keep them in the fridge. Cold temperatures lessen tomato flavour, so eat them at room temperature for a tastier tom.

Tomatoes can be yellow, black, pink and purple. There are thousands of varieties from little cherry tomatoes to big beef tomatoes.

GROWING TOMATOES

Tomatoes are not easy to grow, and you have to mind them all the way from early spring to late autumn, but they are still one of my favourite things to grow. Nothing tastes quite like a home-grown tom, eaten straight off the plant on a sunny day!

This one's a real handful!

	Jan	Feb	Mar	Apr	May	Jun	Jul	Aug	Sep	Oct	Nov	Dec
Sow		✓	✓	✓								
Harvest							✓	✓	✓	✓		

Tomatoes prefer a Mediterranean climate, so that means we have to grow them somewhere warm. Inside the house in a pot, in a greenhouse or a polytunnel are all great options.

Mama mia! This is the life!

GARDENER PHRASE

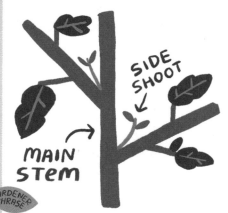

SIDE SHOOT

MAIN STEM

Sideshoots are brand new tomato plants that grow out of the main stem of the plant. In the summer months, we remove these shoots weekly to keep the plant's energy focused on growing lots of lovely tomatoes.

Here's a Know-It-All fact that will blow your mind: grown from a teeny, tiny seed, a healthy cherry tomato plant can produce up to 400 tomatoes in one growing season.

my babies are all grown up!

My favourite variety of tomato is called Sungold, a little red-orange cherry tomato. It's so tasty it's like eating a sweet (but much better for you!).

SOW

When to Sow:
Sow seeds between February and April at 20°C. Fill an 8cm pot almost to the top with seed compost. Give it a few taps on the table to settle down the compost.

How to Sow:
Place 8–10 tomato seeds on the surface, spacing them around 2cm apart. Cover with a little layer of compost (around 5mm) then give it a water.

How to Transplant:
When the seeds have germinated and are 3-4cm tall (about four weeks after sowing), carefully move each one into its own pot or module tray.

When the seedlings look like they are outgrowing their pot or tray, move them on again. This time, either put them into the ground, in a big pot in the greenhouse (a minimum of 30cm wide and deep) or into a growbag.

GROW

GLUG GLUG GLUG

SO Thirsty

Growing Tips:
Tomatoes are thirsty plants and need up to 13 litres of water each week! I also give them a liquid organic feed (you could use the famous comfrey tea from p. 19) every two or three weeks once you see tomatoes starting to grow.

HARVEST

HANDY HACK

If you put a green tomato in a drawer with a ripe banana, the tomato will go red! That's because the banana gives off the ripening gas ethylene.

BIG WOD

When to Harvest:
Tomatoes are ready to eat when they go red, which is usually from July onwards. The lower tomatoes on the plant start to ripen first.

If you have too many green tomatoes, you can use them up by putting them in a chutney. Chutney is a sweet sauce you can eat with cheese and goes very well with Indian food.

BASICS: WATER

Water is really important, as it keeps me and my veggies alive. But we could all do with being more careful with the amount of water we use.

In a country like ours where it rains a lot, we don't need to water much outside in the veg patch. However, with the effects of climate change, some of our summers have been very dry and hot. At these times it's doubly important to try and save our water! In some areas, there is a ban on using hoses during really dry weather, which means we need to have our own supply for watering the vegetables.

MONTY SHeddiNGTON-PoTtS

Why Do Plants Need Water?

Water is really important to plants. Through a process called 'photosynthesis', they use water and CO_2 to make glucose and oxygen. They also use water to transport minerals around the plant in the same way our blood carries important things around our bodies. Since plants don't have mouths to slurp deliciously cold water, instead they absorb water from the soil through their roots via osmosis.

GARDENER PHRASE

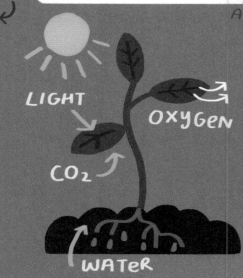

GARDENER PHRASE

PHOTOSYNThesiS

BIG WORD ALERT

LIGHT

OXYGen

CO_2

WATER

A Wet Butt

A water butt is like a big bucket attached to the drainpipe on your house or shed that collects rainwater. The bigger the bucket, the more water you can save! You can collect 24,000 litres of water a year from a standard roof. How do I know? I measured it, of course! Water butts are pretty cheap and they are really easy to install. Why not make it a family project?

Go back to p. 55 to learn how to make your own water butt!

HOW TO WATER PLANTS

It's much better to give plants a good soaking once a week, instead of giving them a little water every day. This is because getting the water down to the roots of the plants takes much longer than you would think. Sometimes I even get down on my hands and knees and stick my finger down in to the soil to check the soil is wet down deep. People think I'm a bit odd! A 'good soak' means two watering cans per square meter!

A GOOD SOAK

Some veggies need more water than others. For example leafy veg like kale and spinach, and fruiting veg like tomatoes and courgettes, all need lots of water. Root crops like carrots and parsnips don't need as much water. In fact you want them to grow down in to the soil looking for water so they will get bigger!

Veg plants have different water needs at different times of their lives. They need careful watering when seedlings and haven't fully developed their roots yet. They also need watering after transplanting and when they are producing flowers and fruit.

TOP 5 TIPS FOR SAVING WATER

If you water your veggies in a hot afternoon the water will evaporate. To get the most from your water, it's better to water either first thing in the morning or in the evening when it's nice and cool.

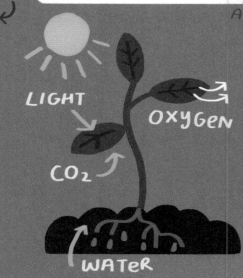 TIME

SOIL

Healthy organic soils are much better at storing water so when we add farmyard manure or compost we're helping conserve water too!

Mulching is where we pile materials like straw, newspaper or compost on top of the soil to preserve the moisture and stop it evaporating. It can reduce a plant's water needs by 50 per cent!

 MULCH

 WEED

Weeds also need water to grow, so by removing weeds you save the moisture in the soil for your veggies.

You can reuse water used for cooking (when it's cooled down) for watering plants.

 REUSE

Plants like tomatoes have very deep roots. Here's a handy trick I've learnt. If you dig a hole beside the tomato plant and put a pot into the hole, you can water into this pot. The water will seep down to the deep roots of the plant.

EAT

IT'S HIGH HARVEST SEASON

There's so much to harvest this month you can skip the supermarket! How about you try ...

mixing a salad with your peppers, cucumbers, beetroot, radish, spring onions, peas, spinach.

→

making jam with your strawberries, gooseberries, blackcurrants, redcurrants.

→

inventing a soup with your cauliflower, cabbage, carrots, turnips, shallots, garlic and broad beans.

HERB HERO

CORIANDER

Did you know?
It's a good idea to ask people if they like coriander before cooking them a meal with it. Some people taste it differently and don't like it because to them it tastes 'soapy'. You can use the seeds, stems and leaves for cooking and eating. In some parts of the world it is called 'cilantro' or 'Chinese parsley'. It can also be used to ease tummy gassiness!

When to sow?
You can sow coriander any time between March and September. I usually sow a little bit of it every few weeks because I love having a constant supply. I sow three or four seeds in each module of a module tray filled with seed compost. It then takes about two or three weeks to germinate.

How to grow?
After four or five weeks, I move it to the ground outside, with plants spaced 20cm apart. You could also transplant the seedlings to a bigger pot filled with potting compost. To harvest, either snip individual leaves or cut the whole plant back with a scissors. If you want to harvest coriander seeds, you will need to let the plant grow and produce flowers.

Tasty in:

Tomato salsa →

Guacamole ↲   Tacos ↑

WHAT'S IN July SEASON

NEW POTATOES

Wrap a bunch of baby new potatoes in tinfoil and season with olive oil, salt and pepper. Bake on the BBQ until cooked, about 15 to 20 minutes.

FRENCH + RUNNER BEANS

Gently steamed or al dente, beans are a sweet summer treat. Cooking reduces their nutritional value so eating them raw is better for you. Plus they're crunchier that way.

AUBERGINE

Chop into disks, grill on the BBQ and serve with a squeeze of lemon, a drizzle of olive oil and a pinch of salt and pepper.

COURGETTE

See p. 53 for delicious courgette recipe ideas.

TOMATO HANDY HACK

Tomatoes will last longer if you store them with their stems pointing down!

CURRY ↙   RICE ↖

60

HOME-MADE KETCHUP

makes 1 jar

Ketchup is a kitchen classic and great with lots of foods, but shop-bought ketchup can sometimes be very processed and high in sugar. However, if you use home-grown tomatoes to make your own ketchup, they'll have enough natural sugar to make it naturally tasty. Here is a simple ketchup recipe:

HELPING HAND

Core and finely chop tomatoes (3 big ones).

Peel and chop a clove of garlic (1).

Drizzle olive oil (1 tbsp) in a saucepan and heat it up.

Simmer the garlic and the tomatoes in the oil over a medium heat.

> **Coring** tomatoes means taking the green tipped, firm centre out of them. I like to leave the seeds in for this recipe, but you don't have to.

Add paprika (1 tsp)
Golden sugar or local **honey** (2 tsp)
Worcestershire sauce (1 tsp) and
Apple cider vinegar (2 tsp).

Season with salt and pepper.

Simmer for 10 minutes over a medium heat and then remove from the heat and allow to cool.

Blitz the mixture in a food processor.

Pour the ketchup into a clean, airtight jar or bottle. You can make your own label with the date on it.

Store the ketchup in the fridge at all times and use it up within two weeks.

The NOT-SO-GREAT POETRY CORNER

Bella Italia FLAG SALAD

Some people think that every salad has to have lettuce as an ingredient, but there are many salads that don't, like Caprese salad. I think this is the most Italian salad there is. It looks a little like the Italian flag with the three colours: red, white and green. It comes from the Caprese region of Italy where mozzarella cheese, tomatoes and basil are local ingredients.

serves 2
← with crunchy bread

> Fresh mozzarella usually comes in a tub or a bag and is stored in a watery liquid which you drain off first.

HELPING HAND

Slice a ball of **fresh mozzarella** into thin slices.

Wash some **large tomatoes** (2) and **fresh basil leaves** (handful).

Slice the tomatoes into thick slices.

Make a row on a plate using the pattern: tomato slice, mozzarella slice and basil leaf. Keep going until you've used up all your slices.

Drizzle the salad with a little **olive oil**.

Season with cracked **black pepper and salt**.

Serve with a little **balsamic vinegar** as an extra dressing to drizzle over the salad when you're eating it.

Buon Appetito!

TOP TOMATO SECRET

They call me the Tomato King, because I grow every breed,
From cherry to beef, I sow my juice bombs from seed.
All the famous chefs use my toms for their passatas,
They won't use anything other than my world-famous 'tomatas'!

Every year it's off to Spain, to 'La Tomatina' I go,
Where I'm begged for my tips on how to grow a great tomato.
When I display my fruits, I glow red, warm with pride,
But I'm afraid my method's Top Secret – tomato classified.

You see there's a secret that no one else knows,
About how I grow my scrumptious tomatoes.
Do I tell them my secret, or keep it under my hat?
Would they laugh if they knew it's doo-doo, that it's as easy as that?

Do I tell them my trick is just pungent horse dung …
Should I share my smelly secret, or do I keep it schtum?
Will someone grow a better tomato? That's my greatest fear.
I think I'll keep it quiet and scoop first prize each year.

AUGUST

Jam season is here! Beat the birds to the early blackberries and keep your eyes peeled for juicy ones on bushes. The early bird catches the worm (and the best blackberries) so be up earlier than the birds. Make haste (hurry up) and make jam but watch out for brambles and nettles.

1	**2**	**3** Try mustard on your sandwich today. Wholegrain, English or Dijon. It's punchy in a cheese toastie!	**4**	**5** Keep your eyes peeled for blackberries growing in your area.	**6**	**7**
8	**9** Raid the recycling and make a berry picking bucket (see p. 63).	**10**	**11**	**12**	**13** Organise a blackberry picking expedition. Watch out for nettles!	**14**
15	**16**	**17**	**18** Write a bad poem today. I like to write a bad poem every day.	**19** Check out my *Not-So-Great Poetry Corner* at the end of every chapter.	**20**	**21**
22 Get ready for going back to school.	**23** See how much you've grown over the summer!	**24**	**25** Have a bean tee-pee hang out with some friends. See p. 63 for how to make one.	**26**	**27**	**28** Start planning your back to school lunch menu. Challenge yourself to try one new lunch every week.
29 Try and add a herb to one of your meals today.	**30** Toast a Marshmallow Day.	**31**	八月 Agosto Αύγουστος **Chinese:** *bah yuweh* **Filipino:** *agostoh* **Greek:** *ahgoostoss*			

HELPING HAND

AND NOW FOR THE WEATHER

Depending on who you talk to, August is either the first month of autumn or the last month of summer. Either way, Ireland experiences average temperatures of a very pleasant 16–19°C during this month. All the more reason why it's so hard to think about going back to school.

By the end of August, days are getting shorter. Sunrise is at 6:30am and sunset is just after 8pm.

In August 1986, Hurricane Charley brought the heaviest rain and worst floods in 100 years to Dublin. A whopping 28cm (almost a ruler length) of rain fell in one day!

GIY LOG BOOK
(NOTHING TO DO WITH LOGS)

This month to SOW:
- ✓ Salad Leaves
- ✓ Salad Onions
- ✓ Chard
- ✓ Spinach

Don't Forget:
- ✓ Lie in a Hammock and CHILL OUT!

This month to HARVEST:
- ✓ Tomatoes
- ✓ Aubergine
- ✓ Cucumber
- ✓ Red Pepper

Other jobs:
- ✓ Water those pumpkins to help them get BIG and FAT!

AUGUST JOBS

August is a month when you get to enjoy the veg patch. We've done most of the hard work, and there's a pause before things get busy with harvesting and making chutneys and preserves next month. So relax and enjoy it. In August GIYers (unlike most people) pray for the odd rain shower so we don't have to water outside! We're funny like that.

GARDENER PHRASE

'Green manure' is the strange GIY name for a plant that we grow just to feed the soil and make it healthy. The roots of a green manure plant grow deep in the soil, helping to break it up and make the drainage better. This is the perfect time of the year to sow many of them – they grow like grass over the winter and then in the spring we chop them down and dig them into the soil. Green manures include clover, vetch and rye.

GARDENER PHRASE

We love sweetcorn in GIY because it is a vegetable that teaches us a lot about how amazing vegetables taste when they are picked really fresh. Each sweetcorn plant will only make about two yellow cobs. We pick them soon after the 'tassels' on top turn brown, and run into the kitchen to cook them while they are perfectly ripe!

TASSEL

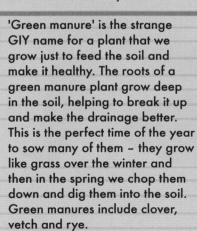

MAKE A BERRY PICKING BUCKET!

GET CRAFTY IN AUGUST

Take any plastic container or small cardboard box you might have in your recycling bin (an old lunch box will do) and get a helping hand to punch or drill a hole in either side.

HELPING HAND

Use an old shoelace to thread through each hole and tie a knot to make a strap you can put over your shoulder and free up your hands while out picking blackberries.

Wear long sleeves and wellies and look out for brambles and stinging nettles. Focus on your work to make sure you don't prick your finger while picking a berry.

HERO OF THE MONTH
GREEN BEAN

Beans were very popular with the Aztecs and Incas in Mexico and Peru. They were growing beans 5,000 years ago. Beans are still a key ingredient in lots of Mexican dishes.

The Greek philosopher Pythagoras was not a bean fan. He believed that they contained the souls of the dead and therefore should never be eaten. His theory was that human souls travelled to the afterlife Hades through the stems of bean plants, so walking near bean plants or even eating them was risky for living souls and could upset the spirits in the beans.

The Story of JACK SPRIGGINS and the ENCHANTED BEAN

The English fairy tale 'Jack and the Beanstalk' was first published as 'The Story of Jack Spriggins and the Enchanted Bean' in 1734.

It's the story of a poor boy farmer who trades his only cow for some magic beans, much to the annoyance of his mother. When he plants the beans, a giant beanstalk grows to the sky. Jack, the curious type, climbs the beanstalk to find a giant's castle in the clouds. The giant, unfortunately, prefers eating people to beans! He smells Jack and wants to eat him as a snack.

We all know the start of the rhyme:
'Fee-Fi-Fo-Fum,
I smell the blood of an English man ... '

But do you know the gruesome lines that follow? Here they are:
'Be he alive, or be he dead,
I'll grind his bones to make my bread.'

I think if someone was threatening to make a loaf out of me, I'd do what Jack did: steal the giant's golden goose and magic harp and cut down the beanstalk!

CLIMBING BEAN TEEPEE

If you are thinking of growing some green beans, why not grow them into a teepee that will also give you a garden getaway to relax in or a clubhouse for your secret garden society? An edible bean tent is simple to make and can be grown in your vegetable patch or even directly on your lawn. This is a project that you can do in May or June, and by August it will be the perfect den.

YOU WILL NEED
- Eight to ten bamboo canes (6ft minimum)
- Pack of bean seeds (runner or climbing French)
- Garden twine

Dig a big bucket of compost or well rotted farmyard manure into the soil where you are going to sow your beans.

Push your bamboo canes into the ground in a large circle (about 1.5m in diameter) and secure the tops of the canes together with the twine to form a teepee. Leave a large gap between two of the canes for an entrance.

In the prepared ground at the base of each cane, sow four bean seeds by making four holes about 5cm deep with your finger. Drop a seed into each hole. Give it a good water.

When they emerge, protect the seedlings from slugs with organic slug pellets or by removing slugs at night-time.

To get the plants started, you might need to wrap them around the canes. The plants will make beautiful flowers and then lovely beans that you can pick and eat. Once fully grown, the leaves of the bean plants will make the perfect den.

BEAN MYTHS AND LEGENDS

DO BEANS MAKE YOU GASSY?

Beans have a bad reputation for being a 'musical fruit that makes you toot'. The reason for this is that they contain oligosaccharides which are complex sugars that our bodies need to work harder to digest, often causing gas. The good news is, if you eat beans regularly you will have less flatulence from them as your body gets used to digesting them. So, don't fear the toots and tuck into those beans.

BIG WORD ALERT

DOES COFFEE COME FROM A BEAN?

Yes, coffee comes from a bean that is then roasted and ground to make coffee granules that you mix with hot water. Vanilla also comes from beans that grow in a pod. So we have beans to thank for ice cream.

CAN YOU EAT BEAN PODS?

Some bean pods are edible, like green bean pods, but it's always best to check that pods are edible before tucking in. The more mature a bean pod gets, the harder and stringier it becomes, so try and harvest edible pods early so you aren't stuck with hard and chewy pods to eat.

MONTY'S KNOW-IT-ALL → STATS ←

Bean plants grow better in spring and summer because they don't like cold temperatures.

Beans are some of the fastest growing plants, and they grow faster than most other vegetable plants.

There are many varieties of bean. Some of the most common beans are: French, pinto, garbanzo (a.k.a. chickpeas), broad, lima (or butter), kidney, cannellini, and black beans

Beans improve the soil they grow in, unlike most plants. Beans have little bumps on their roots called nodules that add nitrogen to the soil.

There are two main types of beans: those that grow in pods and those that grow in shells. Jelly beans do not grow in nature, as much as we might like them to.

Beans are legumes: plants that do not grow their seeds inside fruits but grow them in pods instead.

GROWING BEANS

When we talk about beans in the veg patch, we're talking about three different types of beans: French beans, runner beans and broad beans. There are so many options for jokes it's not even funny. Don't be a **has-bean**. I've **bean** thinking of you. Where have you **bean** all my life? You get the idea.

	Jan	Feb	Mar	Apr	May	Jun	Jul	Aug	Sep	Oct	Nov	Dec
Sow		✓	✓	✓	✓	✓	✓					
Harvest						✓	✓	✓	✓	✓		

The different types of beans (broad, French, runner) all look slightly different, but they are more or less grown the same way: stick a bean in the soil, and it grows into a big plant that produces lots of other beans. Amazing really; one bean turns into hundreds of beans!

BROAD
FRENCH
RUNNER

The runner and French beans can grow really tall (remember Jack and his beanstalk?) — up to 8–10ft. Broad beans are a little shorter, growing to about 3–4ft. All of them look great in the summer veg patch though. Because they grow so tall, I always make a teepee of bamboo canes for runner and French beans before I sow them, so that the bean plants can latch on and grow up them.

POD ✓
BEAN ✗

POD ✗
BEAN ✓

To confuse things a little more, there are also types of French beans called 'dwarf' French beans which don't grow to more than 40cm high – these are great for a small garden.

With runner and French beans, what we actually eat is an immature pod (one that hasn't produced beans yet). If we left it alone and didn't eat the pod it would eventually grow beans inside. When growing broad beans, we don't eat the pod, but we do eat the lovely beans inside.

SOW

FRENCH & RUNNER:

In May or June, sow two seeds 5cm deep at the base of each bamboo cane. Leave 30cm between the canes. If you like, you can sow again in July for an early autumn crop.

← 30cm →

BROAD:

Sow broad beans in February or March, directly in soil. Sow seeds 5cm deep and 15cm apart.

5cm

15cm

GROW

Runner and French beans might need to be tied loosely to the cane at the start, but once they get started they will wind their way up, up, up!

Broad beans are stronger plants, so I usually just make a ring of twine around some canes to stop the plants from toppling over.

I'm all tied up!

Beans don't like competition from weeds, so hoe between the plants every now and then.

BREAK IT UP GUYS!

They don't need much minding, but give them a good watering in dry weather and put a mulch around the plants if it's very dry.

DRY WEATHER FRIENDS

HARVEST

Just like peas, bean plants are nitrogen 'fixers' meaning they take nitrogen from the air and put it in the soil. For that reason, when the plants are finished making beans, we usually leave the roots in the soil to rot to get all the lovely nitrogen into the soil.

PICK ME!

me! me!

NO PICK ME

With French and runner beans, pick the pods when they are small and tasty. As they get bigger, they get tougher and stringy – not so nice. The key is to keep picking because the more you pick, the more beans the plant produces!

One of my favourite things in life is opening a broad bean pod and seeing the fluffy white fleece inside – the comfiest sleeping bag ever!

z z z

BASICS: FRUIT

Fruits can be a little harder to grow than vegetables, but they are even more delicious. Even the smallest garden can have a mix of fruit like apples, pears, plums, strawberries, raspberries, blueberries and rhubarb.

A lot of the fruit we buy in the supermarket has travelled from around the world and is often picked before it's ripe so it will survive the long journey. Unripe fruit doesn't taste great. This is why you will never taste anything quite as delicious as your own home-grown ripe fruit!

MONTY SHeddiNGTON-potts

TOP 5 HOME-GROWN FRUITS:

Apples
Did you know that nine out of every ten apples sold in supermarkets are imported? Even one or two apple trees will provide a huge amount of apples. If you have a small garden, you can even buy miniature apple trees which give a surprisingly big crop!

Plums
When I first started growing, I was surprised how well plums grow here because they seem like such a warm-climate crop. Just one healthy plum tree will give you a big basket of plump, succulent fruit. But will any of them make it to the kitchen? Not likely!

Strawberries
The true taste of summer, strawberries are easy to grow and can even be grown in containers. A strawberry plant will produce good fruit for about three years, and nothing tastes quite like a home-grown strawberry.

Raspberries
Raspberries grow on tall canes and need a little space, but they are my favourite of all the fruit to eat. In GIY we grow autumn-fruiting varieties of raspberries which are a little easier to grow.

Rhubarb
Is it a fruit, is it a vegetable? Does anyone care? Well they should because it's delicious and always the first crop of the year, ready in March or April before everything else. A single rhubarb plant will provide delicious stems for up to ten years!

WILD FRUIT & NUTS

Lots of fruit and nuts grow wild and can be foraged for free. They are often even more delicious than the fruit we grow ourselves. Think cobnuts, rosehips, blackberries and wild strawberries. Only go foraging with someone who knows a lot about the different plants and can tell you what everything is.

I always find it strange that people head to the supermarket in the autumn to buy expensive punnets of blueberries when our hedgerows are bursting with **FREE** blackberries! We've been gathering and eating blackberries since Neolithic times and little wonder – they are full of vitamin C so are a great way to get your body ready to battle winter sniffles.

Blackberries can be frozen for using later in the year or can be made into crumbles, fools (this is a dessert made with berries and cream), jams, chutneys or – my favourite – eaten raw on porridge or granola.

WHEN PICKING BLACKBERRIES, DON'T FORGET:

The ideal time for blackberry picking is September. In fact, in times past it was thought to be bad luck to pick them after the end of September because the Devil had spat (or weed!) on them.

Look for plump, fresh and bright berries. Duller berries are too ripe.

Try to avoid blackberries growing beside roads which might be polluted with car exhaust fumes.

EAT

HANDY BEAN HACK

To keep your green beans fresher for longer, store them unwashed in an airtight container in the salad section of your fridge. If stored this way, freshly picked green beans can last up to a week and stay crunchy. Only wash them when you plan to eat them.

SHOP ON THE PLOT

BEETROOT
Tomatoes
carrots
cabbage
cauliflower
broad beans
French beans
runner beans
Peas
salad leaves
radish
turnip
Potatoes
onions
Courgette
Peppers
aubergine
artichoke
cucumber

HERB HERO

DILL

Did you know?
The seeds, leaves and root of the dill plant can be used for cooking. In the past, people used to give a dill drink to babies to help them with wind. Dill water was also used as a mouthwash to make breath smell better. In some countries, brides put dill and salt in their shoes on their wedding day for good luck. It might have kept their feet smelling nice too!

When to sow?
Most growers think that dill does best if sown direct into the soil but I find it does well starting off in module trays filled with potting compost. Sow three to four seeds in each module of the tray and keep it somewhere warm and sunny.

How to grow?
Transplant around three weeks after it germinates, leaving 15cm between plants in the soil. Dill takes around two months to grow. Water regularly in hot weather. When growing outside you might need to support the plants with a stick. Keep picking leaves to keep the plant productive.

Tasty with:

WHAT'S IN August SEASON

BERRIES & CURRANTS

Jam making is a great way to work together as a family and save the tasty fruits for winter. Why not make jams with the summer fruits you pick this month? In the simplest sense, making jam is the process of boiling and preserving fruit with sugar.

Organise a family blackberry picking expedition and while you're picking berries in the brambles, you can ask your aunties, uncles, grannies and grandads for their favourite fruit jam recipe. You never know, you could have a family jam recipe. Recipes that get handed down from generation to generation are usually the best and if our ancestors hadn't passed down their recipes, we wouldn't be the cooks we are today.

SWEETCORN

Sweetcorn is great when simply grilled on the BBQ. Serve with a little butter, salt and some freshly chopped parsley.

POULTRY

FISH
YOGHURT
yoghurt
PICKLES

68

cheesy BEANSTALKS

makes enough for 4

These easy, cheesy bean snacks take only minutes to make. I guarantee that you will keep all hungry giants at bay by feeding them some cheesy beanstalks today!

Crush garlic (2 cloves)

Line a baking tray with baking paper.

Wash some **green beans** (450g).

Trim the ends off the green beans.

HELPING HAND

Mix parmesan (6 tbsp),
salt (½ tsp),
and the crushed garlic and trimmed green beans in a bowl.

Spread the dressed beans on your lined tray, making sure the beans all have their own space.

Bake for 13 minutes at 180°C, until the beans are crispy and the parmesan has browned. Serve immediately.

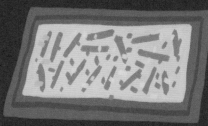

EXTRA mile

If you want to go the extra mile, serve your cheesy beans with **garlic mayonnaise**.

The NOT-SO-GReat POETRY CORNER

GREEN BEAN SESAME SENSATIONS

makes enough for 4

Green beans are used a lot in Asian cooking and are often an ingredient in Thai curries or stir-fries. I like to use sesame oil and seeds when I cook Asian dishes and with green beans, it's sesame-sational!

Wash some **green beans** (500g).

Trim the ends off the green beans.

Crush garlic (3 cloves).

Chop a shallot (1).

Heat a frying pan over a medium heat.

Add sesame oil (3 tbsp).

Add the crushed garlic and shallot and fry them for half a minute before adding your green beans to the pan.

HELPING HAND

Stir your beans in the garlic, shallot and oil, making sure they get nicely coated. Only cook for 5 minutes to make sure that the beans stay nice and firm.

Add soy sauce (2 tbsp) and stir for one more minute, but lower the heat slightly to make sure your garlic doesn't burn.

Serve with a sprinkle of **sesame seeds**. Enjoy!

SIR WILLIAM WINDYBRITCHES OF WINDY ARBOUR

I do love to eat beans for breakfast, lunch and dinner,
Put some beans in your meal and you're onto a winner.
How can one resist them, in burritos, or on toast?
'Beans don't make me windy' I always like to boast.

But when people come over to my house for a party,
They refuse second helpings, fearing they'll become farty.
It's true beans have a bad rep for unsettling the tum,
And causing potent flatulence to fly from the bum.

But how silly to miss out on a delicious bean stew,
For fear of a few parps or toots, so here's what I do:
After beans, I just insist on a tour of my garden,
Where I can parp away freely, and avoid saying pardon.

SEPTEMBER

The leaves may be starting to go brown but don't let that get you down! By now you will have harvested some great crops from your plot and will have home-grown lunches you can impress your friends with.

1 Back to school!	2	3	4 Ask your teacher for homework off to go blackberry picking.	5	6	7
8	9	10 Try a Date Day! They are sweet snacks but watch out for pits!	11	12	13	14
15	16	17	18	19 Collect jars for making blackberry jam ... and for the crafts on p. 71.	20	21 It may be September, but *Oktoberfest* begins in Germany today.
22 HELPING HAND Ask a teacher, friend or relative for a jam recipe and make some with your family.	23	24 Try and buy some local honey.	25	26	27	28 *Nice Neighbour Day.* Help your neighbour take their bins in or ask them over for a meal.
29	30 Go to a local farmer's market.	31				

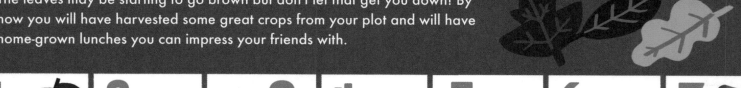

ਸਤੰਬਰ Eylül ກັນຍາ

Punjabi: satabara   Turkish: aylool   Lao: knaia

AND NOW FOR THE WEATHER

It can still be pleasingly warm in September. The highest temperature for the month was recorded in 1906 when it reached a scorching 29.1°C in Kildare.

Days are shortening with just over eleven hours of daylight by the end of this month.

Sunrise is at around 7:30am and sunset is just after 7pm.

In September 1961, Hurricane Debbie brought some of the strongest winds ever recorded and huge damage to Ireland. It travelled all the way from Cape Verde off the coast of Africa, through Ireland and on to Russia!

GIY LOG BOOK
(NOTHING TO DO WITH LOGS)

This month to SOW:
✓ White Turnip
✓ RADISH
✓ SALAD LEAVES

Other jobs:
✓ start making jams, pickles + chutneys from your lovely produce

This month to HARVEST:
✓ CELERIAC
✓ TOMATOES
✓ SWEDES
✓ ONIONS
✓ SWEETCORN

Don't Forget:
✓ If you have a greenhouse or polytunnel — close the door at NIGHT!

GET CRAFTY IN SEPTEMBER

This month you may be collecting jars to put your home-made jams in. If you have any left over, why not use your jam jars to make salt and pepper shakers?

MAKE SALT AND PEPPER SHAKERS!

Try and find two matching jars of a similar size with lids. Smaller jars might save space on your table.

Put a piece of sticky tape over the lid of the jar and mark out your shaker's holes with a marker on the tape. I like to do a circle of holes and usually mark out about eight.

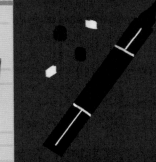

Take a thumbtack or pushpin and pierce the lid where you have marked out your hole pattern. Make sure the holes are pushed the whole way through so they will allow the salt and pepper shake out.

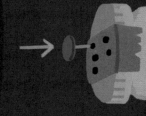

Remove the tape, remove the lid and fill your jars with salt and pepper.

SEPTEMBER JOBS

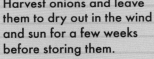

It's still not too late for a bit of seed sowing, but we need to use 'quick growing' veg like baby white turnips, radishes and salad leaves.

Harvest onions and leave them to dry out in the wind and sun for a few weeks before storing them.

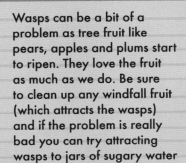

Wasps can be a bit of a problem as tree fruit like pears, apples and plums start to ripen. They love the fruit as much as we do. Be sure to clean up any windfall fruit (which attracts the wasps) and if the problem is really bad you can try attracting wasps to jars of sugary water left near the fruit instead.

As the days get shorter and colder, we don't need to water as much any more. In fact, if you water too much at this time of the year, the leaves of plants can get 'grey mould'. Give pumpkins, squashes, celeriac, runner beans and leeks a good soak once a week if they need it.

HERO OF THE MONTH
SALAD LEAVES

Romaine lettuce, sometimes called Cos lettuce, is a crunchy leaf that is often used to make Caesar salads.

Loose lettuce doesn't grow on a head like other varieties – the leaves simply join at the stem. They can be both red or green.

Mizuna, sometimes called Mibuna, spider mustard or Japanese mustard greens, has a peppery taste and is excellent for adding some excitement to your salad.

Iceberg lettuce got its name from the fact that Californian growers shipped it covered with heaps of crushed ice in the 1920s. Before that, it was called crisp head lettuce. It has a mild taste.

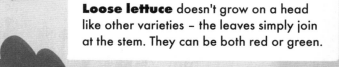

Mustard leaves originated in the Himalayan region over 5,000 years ago. They are broad dark green leaves with a flat surface. This leaf is known for its peppery taste. It's very nutritious and rich in lots of vitamins and minerals.

Rocket has flat, wavy leaves with long stems and, unlike other salad leaves, it has a strong and memorable peppery taste. If you like pepper like I do, then you'll love rocket leaves. In the US it's called arugula.

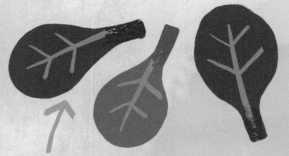

Lamb's lettuce doesn't grow in the shape of a lamb but in delicate clover-like leaves on stems. Some say it got its name because it's the shape of a lamb's tongue. It's more likely that this leaf was a food that lambs liked to eat and so it was named for that reason. It has a mild taste, feels soft and is sold in bunches.

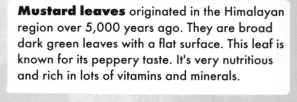

Butterhead lettuce leaves are loosely attached to the head and are a dark green colour. If you feel the leaves they have a buttery texture, and it has quite a mild flavour. It's often used in sandwiches.

Bok choy is an Asian green that has been grown in China for more than 5,000 years. It has a mild flavour and is used in lots of Asian salads, soups and stir-fries. It's sometimes called 'soup spoon' because of the shape of its leaves, or 'white cabbage' which may be because the Cantonese words 'bok choy' translate literally as 'white vegetable'.

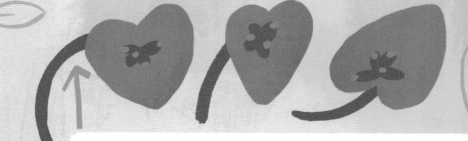

Claytonia is a heart-shaped green salad leaf that tastes a little like spinach. It grows well during cold months and so it's great as a salad ingredient during the winter. During the 1800s in the US, miners ate lots of it to prevent the gum disease scurvy. It's also known as 'miner's lettuce' because of this. Miners worked long hours in the dark and didn't have good diets, so eating this lettuce rich in vitamin C was their way of trying to keep their gums scurvy-free.

SALAD BAR IN A JAR

If you have some jars lying around at home, you can use them to store little snack pack salads in the fridge, ready to grab when you are hungry.

I like to pack the heaviest ingredients at the bottom of the jar, layer by layer, and leave the leaves for the top to keep them from getting soggy.

When I'm ready to eat my jar salad, I add a little lemon juice or salad dressing, seal the jar and shake it before tipping my salad into a bowl to eat.

Light ingredients, like salad leaves and seeds, at the top.

Heavy ingredients, like chickpeas, grains or pasta, at the bottom.

LETTUCE MYTHS AND LEGENDS

DID JULIUS CAESAR INVENT THE CAESAR SALAD?

No! Caesar salad was invented much later than ancient Roman times. The salad was invented by Italian chef Caesar Cardini in America in the 1920s. His kitchen was running low on supplies after the Fourth of July celebrations and he was forced to use whatever he had left to make dishes to serve to his restaurant customers.

ARE DARKER SALAD GREENS MORE NUTRITIOUS?

Yes, dark green lettuce leaves are more nutritious than lighter leaves. Iceberg is said to be the least nutritious as it has very light green coloured leaves.

you look so healthy!

DID PEOPLE ONCE THINK THAT LETTUCE WAS A WEED?

Lettuce was once seen as a weed, until the ancient Egyptians began to plant it on purpose to eat as food. People thought corn salad was just a weed that grew in corn fields until they realised it was edible and tasty and started growing it for salads.

MONTY'S KNOW-IT-ALL → STATS ←

Because salad leaves have such a high water content – over 95 per cent – they don't freeze well. That's why we mostly eat fresh salad leaves and why growing your own is a great idea.

BIG WORD ALERT

The word salad comes from the Latin *herba salta* which means 'salted herbs' which may be because ancient Romans enjoyed eating green leaves dressed with lots of salt.

Because lettuce is mostly made of water, eating lots of it can help keep you hydrated.

73

GROWING SALAD LEAVES

If I ask you to give me a word you associate with 'salad' you would probably think 'lettuce'. But there are far more interesting salad leaves to grow than lettuce! So, as well as lettuce, I grow quick-growing salads with a spicy twist and wacky names like rocket, bok choy, mustard, mizuna and wonk bok (I'm not making that one up).

A REALLY WACKY LEAF

	Jan	Feb	Mar	Apr	May	Jun	Jul	Aug	Sep	Oct	Nov	Dec
Sow	✓	✓	✓	✓	✓	✓	✓	✓	✓	✓	✓	✓
Harvest	✓	✓	✓	✓	✓	✓	✓	✓	✓	✓	✓	✓

SALAD LEAVES ALL YEAR? SUCCESS-ION!

With a lot of vegetables, you sow them once in the year and harvest them later. With salad leaves, you need to be 'succession' sowing. That means you plant a little of them every few weeks. If you're lucky enough to have a greenhouse or a polytunnel, you can grow salad leaves all year around.

Mustard is a delicious salad leaf. The mustard that you eat with your ham sandwich is made by letting the plant grow tall, flower and go to seed, then harvesting these seeds and grinding them down to a paste.

3 MONTHS
3 WEEKS

When growing lettuce, we wait for it to become a 'head' of lettuce before we harvest and eat it. This can take around three months. With leaves like mizuna, rocket and mustard, we can cut them with scissors as early as three to four weeks after sowing! They grow back a second (and even a third) time, which is why they are called 'Cut and Come Again' crops.

GARDENER PHRASE

The Know-It-All secret to an interesting and tasty salad is to get adventurous and think outside the box – or maybe outside the salad bowl. We can also use tender baby spinach, chard, kale, lemony sorrel, foraged leaves like dandelion, and even the leaves from pea or broad bean plants.

LETTUCE:

MUSTARD, ROCKET, BOK CHOY, MIZUNA,

SOW

I sow one seed in each module of a module tray filled with seed compost.

Lettuce seeds need light to germinate, so don't cover them with compost. Keep the compost moist and put the tray somewhere warm and sunny.

2cm

Out in the garden, rake the soil so it's level and flat. Make a shallow drill about 2cm deep and sprinkle the seeds into the drill. Cover with soil and water.

If you have more than one row, make the rows 30cm apart. You can also sow the seeds in containers, sprinkling the seeds on top and covering with a shallow layer of compost.

GROW

20cm

After about three or four weeks in the module tray, plant the seedlings out into the soil or into a larger pot with fresh potting compost. Keep 20cm between plants.

Keep the rows in between the leaves weed-free and water in dry weather (or if you are growing them inside a greenhouse).

HARVEST

Wait until the lettuce has become a 'head' of lettuce to cut. It's best to harvest lettuce in the morning as it keeps longer that way.

What a beautiful morning to be harvested!

Harvest with scissors when the leaves are 10–15cm tall, usually after three or four weeks. Leave about 2cm of the stem, which will grow back later. These leaves can be used in cooking when they are larger.

BASICS: PRESERVING & GLUTS

Every GIYer knows that sometimes when you grow food you end up with a 'glut'. This is when you have more of one type of vegetable than you can eat. We already talked about a vegetable that's more likely to give you gluts than any other – can you remember which one it was? (See p. 53)

MONTY SHeddiNGTON-PotTS

Freeze It

You can freeze veg to preserve it quite happily for four months to a year. Did you know you can freeze peas, French beans, broad beans, runner beans, cabbage, spinach, broccoli, Brussel sprouts, peppers, tomatoes, cauliflower, swedes and carrots? Most veg freeze better if you 'blanch' them first. This means we dunk them in boiling water for a few minutes before draining and then freezing. Enzymes in food that cause it to rot can survive freezing, so by blanching we kill off those enzymes. It also preserves the taste and colour of the food.

HOW TO PRESERVE VEG

GARDENER PHRASE

Pickle It

Putting veg and fruit in jars filled with vinegar (or brine, which is salt water) is one of the oldest ways humans have stored food. Examples are sauerkraut (brined cabbage), pickles of cucumber or green beans, relishes like piccalilli (cauliflower), and chutneys (a combination of fruit and veggies with spices and vinegar).

Store It

You can store some vegetables as they are without freezing, drying or pickling. For example beetroot, turnip and carrots will keep for months in a box of sand. Potatoes can be stored in a box or in hessian sacks. Apples and pears will keep in a cool, dark and frost-free shed. Pumpkins and squash will store quite happily on a shelf somewhere cool. Onions and garlic can be hung in a 'braid' and will keep for up to five months. Some veg can even be stored where they grew in the soil – like celeriac and parsnips.

GARDENER PHRASE

THE GLUTMASTERS

When it comes to glutness (I just made that word up), not all vegetables are created equal. There are some vegetables that just seem to be the glutmasters! Here are our favourites:

Courgette
The number one glutmaster, with one plant producing over forty fruits in a season. I sometimes daydream about new ways to use up courgettes.

French Beans
Try keeping up with a full grown bean plant. Have the freezer at the ready.

Tomatoes
A healthy cherry tomato plant can produce over 300 tomatoes between July and October. That's a lot of tomato deliciousness.

Cucumber
A healthy cucumber plant can produce thirty to forty cucumbers in a season. That's a LOT of tzatziki.

Peppers
From one tiny little seed, a pepper plant can produce literally hundreds of peppers, even when grown in a pot inside the house.

Dry It

Many vegetables, fruit and herbs can be dried. Basically this means we take out the water that's in the veg to stop it from rotting. A dehydrator is a special piece of kit in a kitchen for drying food but you can also dry food in an oven (at a very low temperature so you are not cooking it), hot press or even on top of a radiator. In warmer climates you can dry food in the sun (e.g. sun-dried tomatoes). You could try drying slices of apples, peppers, onions, carrots, berries and bananas.

EAT

SALAD HANDY HACK
Try not to store lettuce leaves near apples or bananas as they will make your lettuce decay faster and turn brown and slimy.

HERB HERO

SAGE

WHAT'S IN September SEASON

ONION
If you find you cry when peeling onions, try and cut your onion but leave the root on, that way less of the onion's scent is released.

APPLES
Stew chopped apple in a small pot with a teaspoon of brown sugar and cinnamon for a lovely topping for breakfast cereals and porridge.

PARSNIP
Parsnips are lovely when roasted in a tin with a little olive oil, salt and rosemary. They are naturally quite sweet and roasting them seals in the sweetness.

CELERIAC
Celeriac is great when roasted in a little olive oil, thyme and salt. Clean and peel you celeriac, cut into chunks and roast in a tray in the oven until the celeriac wedges are tender.

BLACKBERRIES
Don't forget to get out and pick some of these as they'll soon be gone.

Did you know?
In the past, people believed that sage was good for your memory *and* stopped you sweating too much. People believed it was a bit of a miracle cure for lots of things, so much so that its name comes from the Latin word *salvis* which means 'to save'. They thought it was a cure for bleeding gums, sore throats, memory loss and headaches! Sage has greyish green leaves and purple flowers. The leaves (the part we use for cooking) are usually picked when the flowers are in bloom.

When to sow?
The easiest way to grow sage is to buy a little plant in a pot in a garden centre. To grow from seed, sow in March or April in a pot filled with potting compost. Be patient! It is very slow to grow and you won't be able to harvest it until the following year.

How to grow?
Sage will grow well in containers, pots or the soil outside. It loves the sun – a bit like myself. Sage is a Mediterranean herb so it doesn't like waterlogged soil, and you might need to support the plant with a stick. Keep picking leaves to keep the plant productive.

BUTTERY sauces

RICH MEATS

Tasty in:

STUFFING

CREAMY PASTA

TEA PARTY

ROCKET PESTO

I like my pesto to pack a peppery punch, so I make mine using rocket.

Blitz garlic (2 cloves), Rocket leaves (200g), Basil (10g), Sunflower seeds or pine nuts (30g), Parmesan cheese (50g), Lemon juice (1 lemon), Olive oil (80ml) and a pinch of salt and pepper in a food processor until all of your ingredients mix to form a green pesto.

makes 1 jar

Serve with pasta or spread on bread.

Legend has it that tea was first discovered by the Chinese emperor Shennong in 2737 BC. Shennong liked to have his water boiled to clean it before he drank it. The legend goes that one day some wild tree leaves blew into his water as it was boiling, giving flavour to the brew. When he drank it, he was intrigued by the taste! He said he felt that the flavoured drink was warming and investigating every part of his body and so he named the brew **c'ha** which means 'to investigate'.

China has a very strong tradition of tea growing, brewing and drinking to this day and tea ceremonies are a traditional part of their culture. Tea leaves can be brewed loose in water or in tea bags, but did you know you can make your own herbal teas from everyday herbs? Why not host a herbal tea party using some of the herbs you've grown yourself?

STRAWBERRY salad

Because rocket is a peppery leaf, it goes well with sweet berries like strawberries. I like to experiment with nuts and berries as ingredients in my salads and this peppery strawberry salad is one of my favourites.

Steep a generous handful of the leaves of the herb of your choice in a tea pot, allow to brew for 2–3 minutes and serve with a little honey. Easy and delicious!

Toss strawberries (6 chopped), Walnuts or carmelised pecans (8) Sweet cherry tomatoes (6) and Rocket leaves (handful) together in a bowl.

Crumble some goat's cheese through the salad.

Add balsamic vinegar (2 tbsp), Lemon juice (a squeeze) and Salt and pepper to the bowl for a sweet but peppery salad.

Try out all the different herbs in your garden to make a variety of yummy teas:

Lemon Balm leaves make a lovely refreshing, zingy brew.

Mint leaves can make a tea that is nice to drink after a big meal or for bellyaches.

Rosemary and Thyme make a nice brew for sore throats.

The NOT-SO-GREAT POETRY CORNER

makes enough for 1

SWEAT AND FRET THE COURGETTE THREAT

A marvellous veg is courgette,
Lots of fruit you will get,
From one little plant you grow all you need,
Isn't that amazing from one tiny seed?

The first ten courgettes are tasty I'll grant you,
The second ten are pretty good too,
The third ten, OK, the fourth ten a bore,
Oh now I can't eat any more!

I've used every recipe in every book,
Tried a hundred different ways to cook,
In salads and tartlets and tray bakes,
I've even tried eating courgette cakes!

I gave a bag of courgettes to Aunt Betty,
And I'm getting kind of tired of courgetti,
I used a big one to keep open a door,
It dropped on my foot, that was sore!

I can't keep up, it's a nightmare,
How many more can there be out there?
One of them has turned into a marrow
So big it won't fit in the barrow.

OCTOBER

With Halloween just around the corner, watch out for zombies ... courgette-guzzling ones that is! I call them **Zucchini Zombies**. These hungry neighbours are sure to be drawn to your plentiful patch of pumpkins and squashes too!

1 *World Vegetarian Day!* Celebrate with your favourite vegetarian meal today.	**2**	**3**	**4** Taco Day!	**5**	**6** *Mad Hatter's Day.* Wear a mad hat and have a tea party! (Try herbal teas from p. 77.)	**7**
8	**9**	**10**	**11** *World Egg Day.* Buy some local eggs from a farmer's market.	**12**	**13**	**14**
15	**16**	**17**	**18**	**19**	**20** Tell five people a knock-knock joke today. Make it a good one!	**21**
22 *Mama mia!* Have a pasta party!	**23**	**24**	**25**	**26**	**27**	**28** Raid the recycling for the ultimate DIY Halloween costume.
29	**30** Carve a Pumpkin Day.	**31** *Halloween!* Trick, treat and lots of pumpkin to eat.				

十月 Octubre казан

Japanese: *jugatsu*   Catalan: *oktoober*   Kazakh: *qazan*

AND NOW FOR THE WEATHER

Clocks go back in October, and it suddenly feels very wintery. By the end of the month, the sunset happens just before 5pm, and we've only nine to ten hours of daylight per day.

The average temperature is down to 11–13°C, but we can still get occasional hot days. In October 1908 a temperature of 25.2°C was recorded in Kildare!

In October 2017 Storm Ophelia brought wind speeds of up to 156km per hour to Ireland, lifting roofs and felling countless trees.

GIY LOG BOOK
(NOTHING TO DO WITH LOGS)

This month to SOW:
- ✓ Garlic
- ✓ Broad Beans
- ✓ Onions
- ✓ Peas

Other jobs:
- ✓ Take out veg that have finished growing and put them on the compost heap.

This month to HARVEST:
- ✓ Carrots
- ✓ Parsnip
- ✓ Pumpkin
- ✓ Squash
- ✓ Courgette

Don't Forget: cover empty beds to keep them nice and toasty in winter

GET CRAFTY IN OCTOBER

This month we'll be talking about seed saving, so some seed saving envelopes will come in handy.

MAKE SEED SAVING ENVELOPES!

OCTOBER JOBS

October does bring some sowing work in the veg patch, but now we're sowing for next year. The big two this month, for me, are garlic and broad beans. The earlier we plant garlic, the more chance it has of getting the cold weather it needs for the clove to split and turn into a bulb. It needs about five weeks in the soil when the temperatures are less than 5°C. This month we can also sow 'over-wintering' varieties of onions and peas.

GARDENER PHRASE

Don't let all those lovely leaves that are lying around go to waste. If you pile them all into a black sack, punch some holes in it and leave to sit for a year, they will turn into a beautiful type of compost called 'leaf mould'. You can use it to make your soil even more amazing.

GARDENER PHRASE

If you have some leftover beetroot, you can store them in a box of sand. Put a thin layer of play sand in a box. Cut the leaves off the beetroot, leaving just a few centimetres of the stalk on the root. Give them a clean (but not a wash) to get the soil off. Put your beetroot on the sand and cover them with more sand. They should keep quite happily for up to three or four months if you store the box in a dark, cool place like a shed.

Raid the recycling for scraps of old paper you can reuse to make your own envelopes.

Cut some pieces of paper into an even square. I usually make mine about 10 x 10cm. You can adjust the size to suit the size of the envelope you'd like to make as long as it is an even square.

Fold your square piece of paper in half to make a triangle.

Fold the sides into triangular flaps.

Tuck the corner of one flap into the fold of the other to hold it in place.

The top flap of your envelope you can seal with a sticker or a piece of sticky tape once you've put your seeds inside.

Decorate your envelope with markers. You can even draw a picture of the plant on the outside to tell your saved seeds apart.

SEEDS

HERO OF THE MONTH
PUMPKIN

EX-SEED-INGLY INTERESTING!

Pumpkins originated in Central America. Archaeologists have seeds from pumpkin plants in Mexico that date as far back as 5500 BC.

Native Americans preserved pumpkins by drying them in the sun. They peeled the skin, scooped the insides out and sliced the pulp into rings. Then they put them on drying racks to dry in the sun. Drying a pumpkin out makes it last longer.

In the 1500s, a French explorer named Jacques Cartier was exploring North America. He reported finding 'giant melons' on his travels, and so the English word pumpkin may come from the old French word for melons – *pompons*.

The story of Cinderella is thousands of years old, and there are different versions from country to country around the world. It's usually the story of a young girl who overcomes hard times and harsh treatment by others to triumph and live happily ever after. The story most of us know, where Cinderella's fairy godmother turns a pumpkin into a carriage, was first seen in the 1600s.

It's said that dried fruits, boiled pumpkin and turkey were served at the very first Thanksgiving feast in America in 1620. The English pilgrims arrived there in November 1620 and founded the first English settlement called New England. Thanksgiving is celebrated in the US on the fourth Thursday in November every year. It's a feast day that celebrates the giving of thanks for the autumn harvest.

Over 90 per cent of the pumpkins sold in the United States are sold for decoration only, which we GIYers think is a terrible shame. Pumpkins are such a versatile food that can be eaten sweet or savoury in so many different ways. If you are carving a pumpkin into a jack-o'-lantern at Halloween, why not use the pulp to make soup and toast the seeds for salads?

DON'T BE SCARED! EAT MY GUTS!

Here are one of my favourite traditional Halloween games you can make and play at home. I call it:

BOWLS OF FORTUNE

Line up five bowls in a row. Fill one with water, one with soil, one with coins, one with sand and one with a twig. Take turns to put on a blindfold and shuffle the bowls around, then choose a bowl with your hand. Whichever bowl you pick will tell your fortune.

SOIL
You'll have a great growing season, so get planting those pumpkins!

WATER
You will travel overseas soon.

COINS
You will come into money, maybe from selling your pumpkins at the local farmer's market.

SAND
You'll go to a hot place soon, or possibly find pirate treasure!

TWIG
You will climb the highest of mountains.

BIG SNAP challenge

You'll need some string, apples, somewhere to hang the apples and someone to judge who the winner is. Apples are in season, and this is the perfect Halloween game for apple lovers.

Tie a string to the stalks of two apples and hang it from your washing line or the branch of a tree. Prepare one for you and one for a friend. Now, challenge a friend to an apple eating competition. With your hands behind your back, try and eat as much of the hanging apple as you can. Whoever manages to eat their apple first, is the **BIG SNAP CHAMPION!**

PUMPKIN MYTHS AND LEGENDS

CAN YOU EAT ALL OF A PUMPKIN?
You can eat the skin, leaves, flower and seeds of a pumpkin. No waste! If you roast pumpkin then the skin softens and it's easier to eat.

IS THERE MORE THAN ONE TYPE OF PUMPKIN?
Yes! There are more than forty different types of pumpkin.

DO SOME PEOPLE CARVE TURNIPS INSTEAD OF PUMPKINS FOR HALLOWEEN?
Yes! Traditionally in Ireland, turnips have been used for Halloween jack-o'-lanterns for hundreds of years, but pumpkins have become more popular now. It's thought that when Irish people brought this tradition with them to America, they began to carve pumpkins instead because turnips were harder to get there. They're also much harder to carve!

DIA DUIT! I'm The ORIGINAL PUMPKIN.

The story goes that there was a blacksmith named Jack who was doomed by the Devil to roam the earth for ever. He asked the Devil for some light and the Devil gave him a piece of burning coal, which Jack put in a carved turnip and made it into a lantern he carried about with him to light his way. People would put a pumpkin in their window to keep the ghost of Jack away from their homes on Halloween.

MONTY'S KNOW-IT-ALL → STATS ←

Pumpkin is technically a fruit even though we treat it as a vegetable for cooking.

Pumpkin is rich in vitamins A and B, it's high in potassium, protein, iron and fibre and is rich in beta-carotene, like carrots.

Pumpkins are a member of the *Curcurbita* family, which means they are related to courgettes. Vegetables in this family of plants are often called gourds.

Pumpkin seeds can be saved to grow new pumpkins. The average pumpkin has about 500 seeds.

BIG WORD ALERT

GROWING PUMPKINS

Yes, of course pumpkins are great for carving at Halloween, but they are also really delicious to eat and are very good for you too.

EAT ME

	Jan	Feb	Mar	Apr	May	Jun	Jul	Aug	Sep	Oct	Nov	Dec
Sow				✔	✔	✔						
Harvest									✔	✔		

Most pumpkin plants will produce just one or two large pumpkins – think about all the energy the plant needs to make a big pumpkin! At GROW HQ, I grow a variety of pumpkin called Big Max. It produces tiny pumpkins ... Ah no, only joking. It produces truly **MASSIVE** pumpkins that can weigh in at 45kg, which is about as heavy as an octopus! Some other varieties, like Jack-O'-Lantern, produce four or five baby pumpkins.

One of the reasons I love to grow pumpkins is that they last for ages after you pick them because of their lovely thick skins. Mrs Potts loves to keep a couple of pumpkins on top of the cupboard in the kitchen in the autumn, where they will sit quite happily until the following spring.

BIG MAX

Pumpkin seeds are also delicious to eat. When chopping up your pumpkin to eat it, keep the seeds. Clean off any pumpkin flesh, add a sprinkle of oil and seasoning, then bake in the oven for 20 minutes to make a delicious snack.

SOW

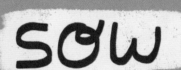

How to Sow:
Fill a pot with compost and sow one pumpkin seed 1.5cm deep.

Keep your pot somewhere warm and sunny (a windowsill inside would be perfect) and keep the compost moist.

SEAWEED DUST

POULTRY MANURE PELLETS

FEED me!

GROW

30–40 cm

When to Grow:
In late May or June, move the seedling to a very large pot (30–40cm deep) or plant outside in the soil.

Though they might not look it at this stage, pumpkin plants grow to be **HUGE** so you need to leave two metres between plants.

Add some poultry manure pellets and seaweed dust to the soil before planting. Pumpkin plants grown in a pot or container need loads of feeding and watering. Give the plant a liquid feed every two to three weeks.

HARVEST

When to Harvest:
Pumpkins should be ready to harvest in October when the plants die back.

After cutting the pumpkin from the plant, leave it out in the sun to dry out for a week or two. This helps the skin to get nice and hard so the pumpkin will store well.

Carefully put a brick or stone underneath the pumpkins to stop them from rotting where they are touching soil.

COMFY!

BASICS: SEED SAVING

When I was a young chap, I read in a book that humans have been growing food for about 10,000 years. This made me wonder; since we've only had shops where people could buy seeds for the past few hundred years or so, where did people get their seeds before that?

In times past, part of the food growing experience included saving some seed to use the following year. Most vegetable plants will produce seed if you let them grow and produce flowers. Saving seed was a way for people to make sure they could grow food the following year, and also to pass on their favourite varieties of seeds to the next generation. It's only in more recent times that the idea of buying seeds from a seed company has become normal. It's very handy, but it also means that the seed companies decide what we can grow, and a lot of the wonderful varieties of veggies have been lost. By saving your own seeds, you can save some money and make sure that you can grow the varieties of vegetables you want to grow.

There are varieties of fruit and vegetables that can only be found in particular countries. These native seeds are as important a part of a country's heritage as its songs, poetry and art. Some countries, including Ireland and the UK, have created seed 'banks' to protect their seeds. I think these seed banks are as important as our museums.

But for me the most important reason to save seeds is to use them to learn more about how plants work. And, besides, it's **FUN**! You get to see the full life cycle of a plant, which begins and ends with seeds.

MONTY SHeddiNGTON-PottS

When saving seed, we first have to know whether a vegetable is an **annual** or a **biannual**. For example, to save seed from a carrot (a biannual plant), you have to wait until the second year for it to produce its flowers and seeds. On the other hand, to save seed from lettuce (an annual plant), we can save seed every year.

> An **annual plant** completes its lifecycle in one year, and a **biannual plant** completes its lifecycle in two years.
>
> *GARDENER PHRASE*

2 YEARS

1 YEAR

LIKE MOTher LIKE Daughter

For saving seed, I generally use **open pollinated** or **heirloom** varieties of veggies. This is because they are more likely to produce seed that is 'true to type', i.e. the same as its parent plant.

GARDENER PHRASE

The good news is that veg plants produce loads of seeds. So, with lettuce again as an example, you only need to let one or two lettuce plants go to seed and you can eat the rest!

GARDENER PHRASE

When lettuce plants 'bolt' or go to seed, the flower heads dry out and have little puffs of cotton at the top. If you pick off these heads and break them apart, you will find a treasure of lettuce seeds inside!

BOLTING

Saving Tomato Seeds

1 Pick a nice big ripe tomato and cut it in half. Squeeze out the seeds, gel and juice (not the flesh) into a cup, and half fill the cup with water. After a few days, mould will form on the water. This mould is a sign that the coating on the seed has dissolved.

2 Pour out the water and any floating seeds (these are duds that won't germinate). The good seeds should be on the bottom of the cup. Rinse the seeds under a cold tap in a fine mesh strainer (so you don't wash them down the sink by mistake).

3 Put the seeds in a single layer on a paper plate and leave for a few days on a windowsill inside to dry out. Bag them up in a labelled envelope and store them somewhere cool, dark and dry until next spring.

RINSE

GIY's TOP 5 SEEDS TO SAVE

1. **SQUASH**
2. **PEPPERS**
3. **BEANS & PEAS**
4. **CUCUMBERS**
5. **LETTUCE**

EAT

PUMPKIN HANDY HACK
When roasting pumpkin, chop it up in chunks and leave the skin on. This makes the skin softer which means that it's easier to eat.

These berries all make great cordials. Cordials are sweet syrups you can mix with water to make a delicious drink.

HERB HERO

TARRAGON

BIG WORD ALERT

Did you know?
It gets its Latin name *dracunculus* because tarragon roots grow back on themselves like a dragon's tail. In the past, people believed the root cured toothache, muscle pain, cuts and bites from animals ... possibly even dragon bites! Tarragon is still thought by many to aid digestion.

When to sow?
It's best to buy tarragon as a young plant in the spring. Tarragon likes well drained soil, so I grow it either in a large pot filled with compost (add in some grit) or planted out in well drained soil.

How to grow?
Grow in a nice sunny spot and keep it well watered, especially if you are growing in a pot. Keep picking off any flowers that appear on the plant. It will die back in the winter and regrow again in spring.

WHAT'S IN *October* SEASON

BEETROOT

See p. 21 for some ideas on how to use your beetroot!

BLACKBERRIES ELDERBERRIES & SLOES

Boil either sloes (750g) or elderberries (750g) with lemon juice (1 lemon) and water (750mls) for 15 minutes on a medium heat until they can be mashed with a potato masher.

Pass your mixture through a sieve, separating the pulp from the juice. Pour the juice and sugar (350g) back into a pan and cook for 10 minutes on a high heat and keep stirring.

Cool and pour the mix into a clean airtight bottle. When you want a refreshing drink, add one part of your cordial to ten parts water (still or sparkling) for a lovely drink.

TURNIP

Steamed and mashed with butter and pepper, turnips are one of my favourite autumn vegetables.

BEANS

Turn to p. 69 for some delicious bean recipes.

CHICKEN

ASPARAGUS

Tasty in:

SALMON

CARROTS

EGGS

PUMPKIN SOUP

makes enough for 4

Pumpkin has such a great flavour that it makes a delicious soup almost on its own, which means it's a really quick and easy soup to make.

Peel and chop some **fresh pumpkin** (800g) into chunks, making sure to remove any seeds. (Keep these for toasting, see recipe opposite.)

Chop onions (2 medium).

Warm olive oil (1 tbsp) in a saucepan.

Fry your onions in the saucepan until they start to soften.

Add your chopped pumpkin and cook for 11 minutes over a medium heat. Stir occasionally.

Season with **salt** and **pepper**.

Add vegetable stock (600ml) and cook for a further 11 minutes.

HELPING HAND

If you want a richer soup, you can go the extra mile and add **fresh cream** (60ml) to the soup and stir through.

EXTRA MILE

Remove the soup from the heat and allow to cool down.

Blitz the soup in a food processor or with a hand blender until it's smooth.

Serve with crusty bread and a sprinkle of toasted pumpkin seeds. I like to add a few dried **chilli flakes** to mine for extra pumpkin punch.

TOASTED PUMPKIN SEEDS

Toasted pumpkin seeds are great as a snack, in salads and as a topping on soups (and even porridge!). If you are carving a pumpkin for Halloween, save the seeds for toasting.

HELPING HAND

Scoop your pumpkin seeds from inside the pumpkin and remove attached fibres.

Wash your seeds well.

Dry using a kitchen towel.

Spread the pumpkin seeds on a baking sheet.

Sprinkle the seeds with olive oil.

Season with a little salt.

Bake the seeds in the oven at 180°C for 45 minutes.

Toss the seeds every 10 minutes to ensure all sides of the seed get baked.

Allow to cool before eating!

THE NOT-SO-GREAT POETRY CORNER

THE HUNT FOR A DEADLY OCTOBER

This is the month when the days get shorter,
Unlike school days which are always torture,
It's when clocks go back and we turn on the heating,
And we stock up on veg for our winter's eating.

This is the month when pumpkins are lit,
And throw strange shadows that scare me a bit,
But their insides taste delish when cooked in a stew,
Go get your own, I'm not sharing with you!

This is the month for tricking 'n treating,
Kids dress up like ghouls and never stop eating,
When they knock on the door, I throw them a courgette,
That's a Monty experience they'll never forget.

This is the month when the dead come to life,
I hope if they're haunting, they go haunt my wife.
Vampires are lurking and mad for feeding,
And while they are at it, they might do some weeding.

NOVEMBER

This month we'll see the days getting shorter and colder. I like to think that there's no such thing as bad weather, just bad outdoor gear. If you have the right rain jacket, woolly hat and boots, you can garden all year round, no matter what the weather!

1 Tally up your treats from Halloween.

2 Take down Halloween decorations.

3 Fill your Halloween pumpkin with bread or nuts and leave outside for birds to snack on.

4

5 Today is Guy Fawkes Night in the UK.

6 Use up any chocolate from Halloween to make chocolate cereal buns.

7 Is it too early to start thinking about Christmas?

8

9

10

11 Still too early to start thinking about Christmas?

12

13

14

15 Have a hot chocolate party.

16 I like to melt a square of my favourite chocolate bar into warm milk to make mine.

17 Bake some homemade bread.

18

19

20

21 Make French toast with beaten egg and leftover bread.

22

23 Try an olive today.

24

25 Only one month until Christmas!

26 *Pest Patrol Day.* Protect your garden from hungry pests that will eat all your veggies.

27 (See the opposite page for a natural pest repellent.)

28

29

30 OK, now you can start thinking about Christmas. Make a list. Check it twice!

Samhain شهر نوفمبر נובמבר

Irish: *sowan*   Hebrew: *november*   Arabic: *sharu nufimbir*

It's getting cold outside. The coldest November temperature ever recorded in Ireland was −11.5°C in Wexford in 2015. Brrr and more brrr!

November can be one of our wetter months. In November 2009, heavy rain brought severe flooding to parts of Ireland, and in Co. Kerry, the rainfall of 360mm was its highest of any month since records began in 1866!

By the end of November, it's dark just after 4pm with daylight lasting for just eight hours a day.

GIY LOG BOOK
(NOTHING TO DO WITH LOGS)

This month to SOW:
✓ **NOTHING!**
(unless you forgot the Garlic last month)

Don't FORGET:
✓ you CAN POT up herbs that don't like the cold, like mint, and bring them in for winter

This month to HARVEST:
✓ APPLES
✓ PEARS
✓ SWEDES
✓ PARSNIPS
✓ CARROTS
✓ CABBAGE
✓ CAULIFLOWER

Other jobs:
✓ Prune apple trees

NOVEMBER JOBS

We're starting to think about next year's growing now, imagine that! We're feeding the soil to replace the nutrients we took from it with this year's growing. A cover of farmyard manure, compost or seaweed would be great. We could also cover the beds with a layer of black plastic or cardboard to keep them nice and snug for winter.

a very SNUG Bed

Early frosts can start to kill off some of our veg that are still in the ground, so it's a good idea to get them out of the soil and into storage. I harvest any beetroot, turnips, potatoes and carrots that are left in the soil and store them in the shed. Hardy parsnips and celeriac, on the other hand, can be left in the soil for the winter.

TO the shed!

If you're lucky enough to live by the beach, you can forage for seaweed to put on your veg beds. Never pull seaweed off the rocks where it's alive. We only pick the seaweed that's washed up on the beach – the day after a storm is a great day for seaweed foraging! Some people say that you should wash seaweed before adding it to the soil. Here's a Know-It-All tip: I think the salt in the seaweed might help keep slugs away from my veggies, so I never wash it!

GET CRAFTY IN NOVEMBER

MAKE GARLIC INSECT REPELLENT!

HELPING HAND

Blitz two whole bulbs of garlic in a food processor (you can leave the skin on) with a few tablespoons of water.

Put the garlic mixture in a 500ml bottle and fill it with water. Seal the lid and shake. Leave the mixture for a few days to brew.

Raid the recycling for an old spray bottle that you can clean out and reuse.

Pour your mixture into the spray bottle and head to the garden to spray any plants that are infested with insects.

Sometimes I spray this on myself to keep mosquitos away on holidays, but it's a bit of a human repellent too!

HERO OF THE MONTH
GARLIC

There is a folk tale in Korea about a bear that became a woman when it was fed twenty garlic cloves a day for 100 days. Can you imagine the bear-woman's breath after eating all that garlic?

Ancient Egyptian pharaohs are believed to have fed garlic to the slaves who were building their pyramids in Giza. This is because they thought garlic would give them the strength and stamina they needed to endure the hard and long work days.

Greek soldiers and Olympic athletes were often given lots of garlic before battles or competitions to improve their performance. Roman gladiators rubbed garlic into their muscles to make them strong for fighting in the arenas. Ancient Greeks and Romans believed that garlic could repel scorpions as well as treat dog bites and leprosy.

GARLIC TONIC III

Bram Stoker, a writer who lived in Dublin, introduced the vampire in his book *Dracula* in 1897. The vampire is an immortal creature who drinks the blood of humans. In the book, the character Van Helsing uses garlic to repel the vampire. Stoker may have got this idea from the fact that people believed that garlic was a mosquito repellent at the time, and I suppose mosquitos are bloodsuckers too!

There were some folk beliefs in Central Europe about garlic being used to ward off evil spirits and werewolves. People often hung garlic in windows and rubbed it on the doors of their home to prevent ghouls and diseases entering. People who are afraid of garlic suffer from 'Alliumphobia'. Do you think Dracula had alliumphobia?

Pee-ew!

BIG WORD ALERT

It's like looking in a mirror...

It's said that the city of Chicago in America got its name from *chicagoua*, the Native American word for the lovely wild garlic that grew in the area.

The English word 'garlic' may have come from the old English words 'gar' meaning spear and 'lec' meaning leek, which meant *spear-shaped leek*. This may have been their way of describing the shape of a garlic clove (which looks a little like a spearhead) and their oniony smell. In fact, garlic, leeks, and onions are all related.

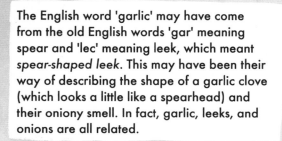

In 1858, Louis Pasteur, who invented pasteurisation, discovered that bacteria cells died when they were doused in garlic oil. This led him and other scientists to believe that garlic had antibacterial powers. During the Second World War, garlic was given the nickname 'Russian penicillin' because Russian soldiers used crushed garlic as medicine when they ran out of antibiotics.

GARLIC & HERB INFUSED OLIVE OIL

Flavoured oil is lovely with crunchy bread or on salads. I make my own infused oil to bring to parties too. Here's a simple way to make roasted garlic and rosemary oil.

1 Top and tail six cloves of garlic.

2 Pour 300ml of olive oil in a baking dish. Add your garlic and three sprigs of rosemary.

3 Cover the baking dish with parchment and bake in the oven on a high heat for 30 minutes.

4 When your mixture has cooled, remove the cloves and rosemary with a spoon and pour your flavoured oil into a clean, airtight bottle or jar. Write the date on your container and use within two weeks.

HANDY HACK!
If you want to get the smell of garlic off your fingers, rinse your hands under some cold, running water while rubbing your fingers with something made from stainless steel, like a spoon. You'll be amazed at how the smell disappears.

GARLIC MYTHS AND LEGENDS

CAN YOU MAKE GLUE FROM GARLIC?
Yes, the sticky juice in garlic cloves is often used as a natural adhesive for repairing delicate glass items and porcelain antiques.

DOES LEMON JUICE GET RID OF GARLIC BREATH?
Drinking lemon juice or sucking on a lemon slice can help stop garlic breath. Chewing parsley can also help.

IS GARLIC POISONOUS FOR DOGS AND CATS?
Yes! Dogs and cats shouldn't eat garlic as it can be very toxic to them.

MONTY'S KNOW-IT-ALL → STATS ←

Garlic can be eaten raw or cooked.

It's estimated that over two-thirds of the world's garlic is produced in China.

Garlic, onions, leeks and chives are all from the same family.

Garlic plants produce greenish white or pink flowers.

Garlic is a bulb that grows underground. Most bulbs will have between seven and fifteen cloves.

Garlic is a good source of vitamin B6. It's also a good source of vitamin C and minerals such as phosphorous, calcium, potassium, iron, and copper that you need in your diet.

GROWING GARLIC

Garlic is where it all started for GIY, so of course we grow loads of it at GROW HQ. Garlic Mick is pretty obsessed with it still, and **VERY** particular about it! Since most of the garlic available in supermarkets is from China (still, grrrr), it's a great one to grow yourself.

	Jan	Feb	Mar	Apr	May	Jun	Jul	Aug	Sep	Oct	Nov	Dec
Sow										✔	✔	✔
Harvest						✔	✔					

Take a bulb of garlic, break out the cloves and stick a clove into the ground. It magically turns into a bulb of garlic after six months. Yes, it really is that simple!

Even though we think about garlic as a Mediterranean vegetable (and it does feature a lot in Mediterranean cooking), it actually likes the cold.

Garlic needs the temperatures to be less than 5°C in order to grow. After about five weeks in the soil, the clove will split and turn into a bulb. Garlic is traditionally sown in December before the shortest day of the year and harvested in June before the longest day of the year.

Garlic can be hung up in a plait or braid when it's harvested, which looks really cool in the kitchen. The garlic should be very happy like this for about six months, and you can just chop off a garlic bulb when you need it.

SO EASY!

TURN DOWN THE HEAT

OOH LA LA

SOW

When to Sow:
Sow between October and December in a sunny part of the garden, giving the soil a feed with some magic seaweed dust and poultry manure pellets before sowing.

yum...

30cm

How to Sow:
Sow by pushing each clove down in the ground with the tip of the clove just below the surface, about 10cm apart in the row.

If you have more than one row, you need to keep the rows 30cm apart so that the garlic has enough space and nutrition in the soil to grow.

GROW

There is very little to do with garlic once it's sown, but it really doesn't like weeds …

WHAT ARE YOU DOING HERE?!

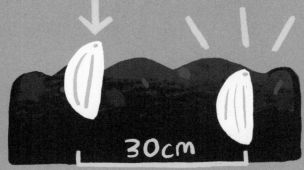

So keep your garlic's bed weed-free while the garlic is growing. Do this by hoeing carefully around the bulbs every few weeks.

HARVEST

When to Harvest:
Harvest when about half the leaves on the plant are yellow, usually in late June or July.

Carefully dig the bulbs out of the soil with a fork.

You can eat them at this stage, but to store them we have to dry them out a little. I leave them on a rack in the garden for two weeks, so the sun and wind can get at them. Then we bring them inside to store.

BASICS: PESTS

It's a fact of life that when you grow your own food, there are insects, birds and animals that love to eat the food too. In many cases they will eat them before you do, which can be ... let's face it ... annoying. I don't really like the word 'pests' to describe them because it's so negative. In fact, many of the insects and bugs in the garden are helping us to grow – we probably couldn't grow anything much at all without our friends the earthworms for example. So even though, yes, there are some 'pests' that love to eat our veggies, they are part of life, and I don't think we should be too cross with them. After all, they are just trying to stay alive. Having said that, I do spend some time (in good humour) trying to outwit them just a little bit! So my top two pieces of advice for budding GIYers are:

1. Work with nature, not against it. Grow some extra veg so that you don't mind too much if slugs munch on some of them.
2. Encourage natural predators into your garden who can help keep it all under control.

MONTY SHeddiNGToN-PoTTS

Pesky VEG PATCH Pests

Rabbits
Rabbits can be a real menace in the veg patch, digging into beds and nibbling on the veggies. A fence around the veg patch can be the only way to really keep them out.

Carrot Root Fly
The carrot root fly is a strange little insect that **LOVES** carrots. If you are working with your carrots between April and August, somewhere a female carrot root fly stops what it's doing, sniffs the air and heads in your direction at top speed! It lays its eggs at the top of the carrot in the ground, and then the little larvae eat their way into the roots. Again, the best protection is to net the carrots. Interestingly, the carrot root fly can't fly above 50cm high! So carrots grown in raised beds seem to be safer from them.

Birds
Pigeons can be a bit of a problem in city gardens (which GROW HQ is), and they love the brassica plants in particular. Other birds go mad for fruit like strawberries. Netting over the plants is the only real way to stop them.

Cabbage White Butterfly
It's a lovely sight to see the white butterflies fluttering around your veg garden, but they are on the lookout for the brassica plants (e.g. cabbage, kale, Brussels sprouts, etc.) to lay their eggs on. These little yellow eggs turn into caterpillars that will devour the leaves of the plants in no time. The best way to stop them is to put a netting over the plants.

Slugs
There can be tens of thousands of slugs in a veg bed, and they are born to eat leaves. In fact, they have 27,000 sharp teeth that can munch quickly through your lettuces, and they leave a special scent trail in the soil so they can make their way back to the same spot night after night! Check out the slug hacks below.

VEG PATCH FRIENDS

It's not all bad. There are some insects in the garden that can actively help.

WORMS
Apart from me, worms are the hardest workers in the garden! As they burrow, they eat soil and decomposing organic matter. It travels through their digestive system and comes out the other end more nutritious and crumbly. They also improve soil drainage by making lots of aerating tunnels through it.

BEETLES
The common ground beetle is a predator for slugs as it eats the eggs. If laying traps for slugs, make sure not to trap the beetles as well.

BIRDS
Some birds help us in the garden by eating slugs and caterpillars. On the other hand, they also eat lots of worms, which is perhaps not so helpful.

BEES
Of course we know by now how important bees are to pollinate the plants in our gardens. Without them, we would struggle to grow food at all.

LADYBIRDS
The larvae of ladybirds can eat hundreds of aphids, and the adult ladybird eats blackfly who munch on broad bean plants.

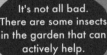

TOP SLUG HACKS

Put a barrier of things that slugs don't like to crawl over around valuable plants like a courgette seedling, for example. Slugs don't like abrasive or sharp things, so they won't crawl over crushed eggshells or grit.

Go slug hunting. Slugs come out to play at night-time, so I go out with a torch in the spring to pick slugs off the leaves of plants. There are other ways to catch them. For example, cut an orange in half and take out and eat the insides. Take the empty skin, poke a hole in the bottom and place it upside down on the soil. Slugs will crawl in there to sleep during the day, and you can pick them off, move them far away from your veg patch or feed them to hens.

Slugs don't like **copper** and get a type of electrical shock off it. You can buy copper tape in garden centres and put it around your valuable seedlings.

Do not be tempted to buy **slug pellets** to kill slugs; they are generally very toxic and bad for your soil. Instead, you could use organic slug pellets that are made from iron. This type of pellet breaks down harmlessly in the earth

EAT

GARLIC HANDY HACK
Many people keep garlic in the fridge, but garlic actually does best when stored at room temperature.

SNIP SNIP!

Sometimes the ends of the artichoke petals have thorns on them. These can be easily snipped off with a kitchen scissors.

HELPING HAND

HERB HERO →

MARJORAM

Did you know?
We use marjoram leaf for cooking with, but in the past, people used marjoram to freshen breath, aid digestion, cure seasickness and soothe sore throats. Sometimes dried marjoram leaves were ground up and sniffed to clear blocked noses! (Don't try this at home - you'll blow the nose off yourself!) Brides and grooms in Ancient Rome wore crowns of marjoram on their wedding days.

When to sow?
Because it lasts for years and years, it makes sense to buy a little marjoram plant from the garden centre, but you can grow it from seed too. Sow a few seeds about 1cm deep in a little pot filled with compost in March or April. Keep it indoors and water when needed. When it's large enough to handle, transplant each little seedling into its own pot with fresh compost.

How to grow?
You can keep the pots indoors until early summer and then plant out into a sunny, sheltered spot in the garden. It will also grow well in a container or large pot.

WHAT'S IN November SEASON

ARTICHOKE
Artichokes might look like a lot of work to prepare, but they're worth it. First, wash your artichoke and slice off the top quarter.

You can then steam the artichoke whole in a steamer or bake in the oven for 30 minutes on a high heat.

When cooked, pull off the outer leaves (we don't eat these). Inside, at the base of the petals, you'll find the tasty artichoke heart!

LEEKS
Leeks are great in soups and mixed through mash.

KALE
Kale doesn't need much cooking and goes very well in mash. It's also great in green juices if you want to blitz it in a blender with some apple juice and spinach.

CARROTS
Make a tasty carrot slaw by grating your carrots and tossing them with chia seeds, raisins, flaked almonds, lemon juice and apple cider vinegar or oil.

WINTER CABBAGE
Winter cabbage is delicious when shredded and cooked in a shallow pan with a little water, butter, salt and pepper and a spoon of wholegrain mustard.

Tasty in:

← FISH

← LENTILS + BEANS

VEGETABLES → MEAT →

garlic mushrooms on TOAST

If you don't know your porcini mushrooms from your shiitake mushrooms, best leave it to the experts and buy some local mushrooms you know are safe to eat. One of my favourite weekend treats is to take time out to pick some mushrooms and make a signature brekkie of garlic button mushrooms on toast. It's a great way to start a Saturday.

Wash mushrooms (500g) with just a light sprinkle of water and pat dry with a paper towel.

Crush garlic (5 cloves).

Chop fresh parsley (3 tbsp) Fresh thyme leaves (1 tbsp) and a Shallot (1).

Mushrooms can soak up a lot of water and get soggy and lose their taste if you let them soak in water for too long.

mushroom memo!

HELPING HAND

Heat some **olive oil** in a pan.

Cook the chopped shallot in the pan for 3 minutes on a medium heat.

Add the whole button mushrooms and cook for 4–5 minutes until brown.

Stir in the crushed garlic and herbs and cook for another 2 minutes on a lower heat.

Toast some **bread** and **butter** it.

Serve your garlic mushrooms on toast with some grated **parmesan** on top.

makes enough for 4

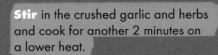

GARLIC AIOLI

makes 1 jar

I love garlic mayonnaise! It's a great dip for home-made vegetable chips and goes well as a dip for garlic breads and pizzas. Aioli is a thinner mayonnaise-based dip, with an extra garlic punch. Saying you made some 'aioli' sounds a little fancier if you want to impress guests.

Crush garlic (3 cloves) and put into a bowl.

Add salt (½ tsp), Mayonnaise (6 tbsp), Olive oil (2 tbsp) and Lemon juice (a squeeze) to the bowl.

MAYO

Mix with a fork or small whisk.

Season with salt and pepper.

Keep in the fridge in an airtight container until you're ready to serve it up. It's delicious paired with breads, pizzas or with raw vegetables as a dip. Use within three days.

The NOT-SO-GREAT POETRY CORNER

HOW DO I LOVE THEE? LET ME CARROT THE WAYS

The carrot root fly is a strange kind of thing,
Doesn't buzz or do insect things, doesn't even sting,
It's not very well known, not really a hit,
This is the first poem written about it.

Fifty centimetres is the highest it can fly,
So you couldn't call it an adventurous guy,
It's never been to the top of a tree,
Never soared high, just as high as your knee.

Doomed to a life flying near to the ground,
Has no special noises, doesn't make a sound,
It's teeny, it's tiny, it's barely recognisable,
But the damage it does can be awfully sizeable.

For there's one thing for which the carrot root fly is known,
A foible, an obsession, a thing all its own,
It has one true love, one reason for living,
If you're growing carrots, that's where it's heading.

It can smell the carrots 10 miles away,
It's determined to find them, will fly all day,
It's obsessed with that lovely carroty scent,
A sniff in the air and off the fly went.

Carrots it lives for, carrots are its loot,
It lays its eggs at the top of the root,
The larvae find the carrot ever so chewy,
And bore in to the centre making them gooey.

93

DECEMBER

The biggest dinner of the year is just a few weeks away so set aside your best vegetables for the big feast. I like to get all my gift-wrapping done early at the start of the month to get a clear run at the month, leaving me more time to plan my Christmas menu.

1 Eat a red apple today.	2	3	4	5 Help someone make a winter fruitcake today.	6	7 Start collecting scraps of paper, magazines and old cards for your junk journal (see next page).
8 Enjoy a day out in town.	9 Make some crafty Christmas cards.	10	11 Put some cloves in an orange and leave it near your radiators to spread a lovely festive smell around your home.	12	13	14 Don't forget to post out your Christmas cards to your friends and family.
15	16 Warm some apple juice with a sprinkle of cinnamon for a lovely winter warming drink.	17	18	19	20 Wrap up some presents today.	21
22	23 Pick out what movies you'd like to watch over the holidays.	24 Hang up a stocking.	25 Christmas Day! Enjoy a family feast.	26 See what creative recipes you can come up with to use up yesterday's leftovers.	27	28
29	30	31 New Year's Eve. Enjoy the countdown and sing 'Auld Lang Syne' with friends and family.	Prosinec Czech: prosinetz	Joulukuu Finnish: yolookoh	십이월 Korean: chibi wie-ay	

AND NOW FOR THE WEATHER

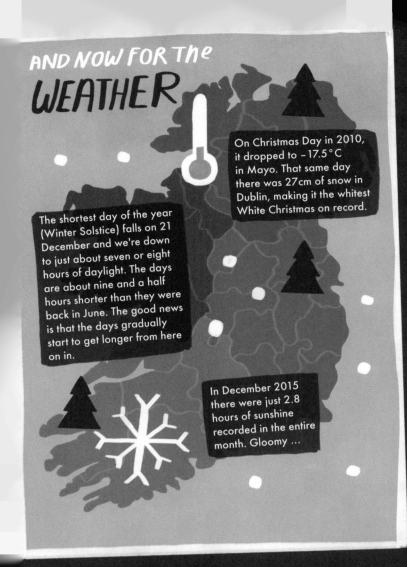

On Christmas Day in 2010, it dropped to −17.5°C in Mayo. That same day there was 27cm of snow in Dublin, making it the whitest White Christmas on record.

The shortest day of the year (Winter Solstice) falls on 21 December and we're down to just about seven or eight hours of daylight. The days are about nine and a half hours shorter than they were back in June. The good news is that the days gradually start to get longer from here on in.

In December 2015 there were just 2.8 hours of sunshine recorded in the entire month. Gloomy …

GIY LOG BOOK
(NOTHING TO DO WITH LOGS)

This month to SOW:
- ✓ NOTHING! you deserve a holiday.

Don't Forget:
- ✓ ENJOY your DOWN TIME

This month to HARVEST:
- ✓ Brussels Sprouts
- ✓ Winter Cabbage
- ✓ Parsnips

Other jobs:
- ✓ Get seed catalogues and order next year's seeds

MAKE A JUNK JOURNAL!

GET CRAFTY
IN DECEMBER

People like to buy planners and diaries as gifts, but why not make your own from recycled bits and pieces? You'll need to be planning what you'd like to grow (and when) for the year to come, and a junk journal is the perfect place to keep track o all your plans.

You'll need to raid the recycling and gather some old ribbons, wrapping paper, cereal boxes, magazines and scraps of paper.

Cut a rectangle from a cereal box and fold in half like you are making a card. Cover the cereal brand side with some paper using sticky tape or glue.

Decorate the front of your journal with cut-outs from your favourite magazines. I use gardening magazines and newspapers to create a collage on the front of my journal.

Gather some sheets of paper (a few pages for every month) and cut them to the size of your journal cover. Fold in half and get help to staple or glue them inside.

Cut a small slit on the front and back cardboard cover of your journal, thread some ribbon through and tie together to close your journal.

You can decorate a page for every month and draw out a daily tracker for all the jobs you need to do that month.

DECEMBER JOBS

Because it's so busy in the garden during the summer, I often take my summer holidays in December. I'm a little strange like that. It's the quietest time of the year in the vegetable garden, and so a nice time of year to take time off to recharge the batteries.

NO-SUN BLOCK

Before I do, we usually do a clean-up in the tool shed, potting shed and greenhouse. We wash the plastic on the polytunnel, clean the glass in the glasshouse and give all the tools a good cleaning. Module trays will last longer if you give them a rinse in the winter. We also keep a close eye on any veggies that we have stored in the shed – throwing out any that have started to go bad.

Even though it's winter, there's still plenty to eat and the 'Hungry Gap' is still months away. We're still enjoying lots of produce straight from the ground like parsnip and celeriac, and veg from storage like onions, squashes, pumpkins, potatoes, beetroot and carrots. We're also still able to grab a jar of chutney or pickle from the larder, or peas, beans or tomato sauces from the freezer.

GARDENER PHRASE

FROZEN PEAS

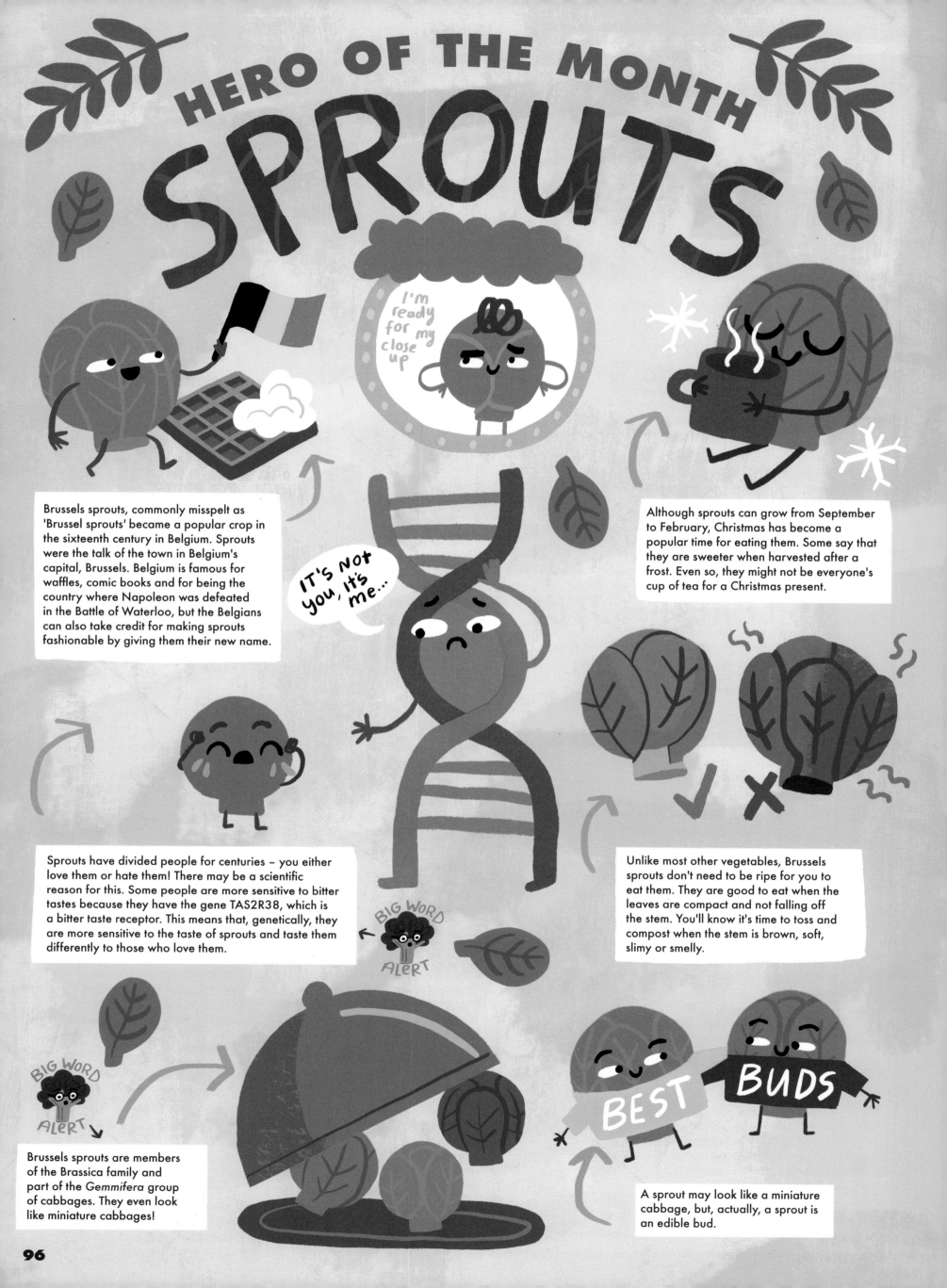

HERO OF THE MONTH
SPROUTS

Brussels sprouts, commonly misspelt as 'Brussel sprouts' became a popular crop in the sixteenth century in Belgium. Sprouts were the talk of the town in Belgium's capital, Brussels. Belgium is famous for waffles, comic books and for being the country where Napoleon was defeated in the Battle of Waterloo, but the Belgians can also take credit for making sprouts fashionable by giving them their new name.

Although sprouts can grow from September to February, Christmas has become a popular time for eating them. Some say that they are sweeter when harvested after a frost. Even so, they might not be everyone's cup of tea for a Christmas present.

Sprouts have divided people for centuries – you either love them or hate them! There may be a scientific reason for this. Some people are more sensitive to bitter tastes because they have the gene TAS2R38, which is a bitter taste receptor. This means that, genetically, they are more sensitive to the taste of sprouts and taste them differently to those who love them.

Unlike most other vegetables, Brussels sprouts don't need to be ripe for you to eat them. They are good to eat when the leaves are compact and not falling off the stem. You'll know it's time to toss and compost when the stem is brown, soft, slimy or smelly.

Brussels sprouts are members of the Brassica family and part of the *Gemmifera* group of cabbages. They even look like miniature cabbages!

A sprout may look like a miniature cabbage, but, actually, a sprout is an edible bud.

A SPROUT'S STANZA

— BY —
RUSSELL SPROUT

THERE ARE PEOPLE WHO'D RATHER
KISS A WET BADGER'S SNOUT,
THAN SINK THEIR TEETH INTO
A BOILED BRUSSELS SPROUT.

I BLAME THEIR TASTE BUDS,
BUT IT COULD BE THEIR GENES,
'COS IF COOKED RIGHT SPROUTS ARE
THE TASTIEST GREENS!

> A certain sprout we know may have thought he wasn't going to get a spot in the book, but Christmas isn't Christmas without a sprout.

SPROUT MYTHS AND LEGENDS

DO BRUSSELS SPROUTS SMELL BAD WHEN COOKED?
Yes, it's true! Overcooking Brussels sprouts can produce a sulphur-like eggy smell, which can turn some people off eating them.

> If you don't like sprouts, maybe you just haven't been cooking them correctly.

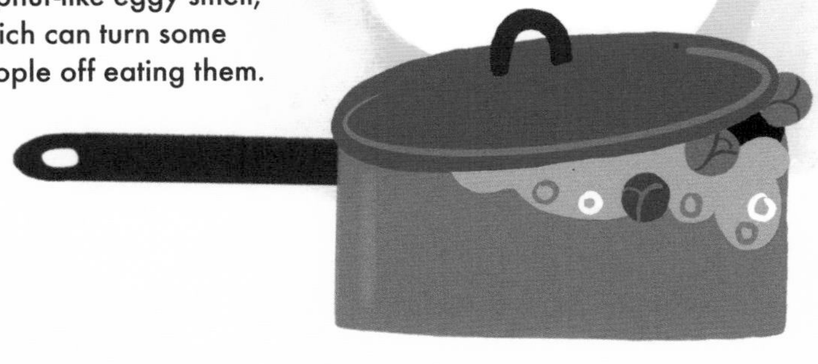

DOES CARVING AN X INTO A SPROUT HELP IT COOK?
Yes! If you gently steam your sprouts and carve an 'X' in their stalk before cooking, they will cook perfectly.

> X marks the spot!

MONTY'S
→ KNOW-IT-ALL →
→ STATS ←

Although their name comes from the Belgian capital, it's the Dutch who export the most Brussels sprouts. They export about 40 per cent of the world's supply!

We're used to the green kind, but purple sprouts are available too! They are grown as hybrids between red cabbage and normal Brussels sprouts.

Brussels sprouts are rich in calcium, potassium and vitamins C, A and K. They really bring a lot to the table!

GROWING SPROUTS

Nothing divides quite like the Brussels sprout (sorry Russell). Some people **LOVE** them (and they are certainly a very healthy, tasty thing to eat in my view) but some people actually **LOATHE** them.

	Jan	Feb	Mar	Apr	May	Jun	Jul	Aug	Sep	Oct	Nov	Dec
Sow										✔	✔	✔
Harvest						✔	✔					

Pest Proofing

Brussels sprouts are hard enough to grow well because, like all the brassica family, they are much loved by caterpillars and other pests.

They also take up quite a deal of space in the veg patch for eight months of the year. But thankfully, if you stick with them, they can give up to 2kg of sprouts per plant in the leaner winter months.

It's Hammer Time

At the end of the season, you can take the plants out of the soil and put them on the compost heap. Given how big the stems are, get a helping hand to smash the stems up with a hammer before composting. Otherwise it would take forever to break down.

HELPING HAND

Sprout Cooking Tip

Don't boil the goodness out of your sprouts when cooking. Cut them in half, blanch them for a few minutes in boiling water and then fry them in some butter with a little chopped garlic.

yum

SOW

We start them off in module trays indoors – sowing one seed per module 2cm deep. You can sow sprouts a couple of times between March and May so that you will have a longer harvest.

Sprouts need good fertile soil. The previous winter, add lots of manure or compost to the soil. Then, before sowing, add a sprinkle of poultry manure pellets and seaweed dust.

SO MANY SPROUTS

Bear in mind that four plants in total is probably enough for most families.

GROW

The seedlings will be ready to transplant from their trays about 4–6 weeks after sowing. Space plants at least 60cm apart. It might seem weird with such a small plant, but they will need that space when they get bigger.

60cm

Carefully covering the plants with a fine net will prevent cabbage white butterflies from laying eggs on the plants. Check the leaves and remove any caterpillars regularly.

HARVEST

Harvest your sprouts from the bottom of the plant first as soon as they look ready to eat. Pull the sprout downwards to snap it off the plant.

The leaves at the top of the stems can be cooked like spring greens – very tasty they are too!

BASICS:
PLANNING & CROP ROTATION

'Crop rotation' sounds complicated, but it's a very simple thing really; we simply group vegetables that are similar together and move them around each year in the veg garden.

← GARDENER PHRASE

The point of it is to try and stay ahead of any pests that might be in the soil and to help keep the soil healthier. Since organic growers don't like using chemicals to kill off pests or to feed the soil, crop rotation is one of the most important parts of organic growing.

Let's take an example. Wireworm in the soil love to crawl inside potatoes and eat them. If you grow potatoes in the same spot year after year, the wireworm will think: 'This place is amazing, there are endless supplies of food. I'm going to set up house here and start a family!'. By growing potatoes in a different part of the veg garden each year, you stay ahead of the wireworm!

MONTY SHeddiNGTON-PoTTS

PLANNING Where To Put your Patch

When you're starting to grow your own food you might have to decide where to put your veg patch in the garden. Of course, it's possible that you won't have any real choice in that, but if you do, here are some **things to consider:**

MAKING A CROP ROTATION PLAN

At GIY we have a good way of remembering where we have to grow everything. We call this our **'crop rotation plan'**. We have five veg groups and five areas in the garden. Everything gets switched around each year: group one starts in area one, then moves on to area two in year two, and so on. Group one won't end up back in area one until the sixth year. Still with me? Good. The five veg groups are:

POTATOES	LEGUMES	BRASSICAS	ONIONS	ROOTS
potatoes	peas, broad beans, french beans, runner beans	kale, cabbage, turnips, cauliflower, sprouts, broccoli,	onions, garlic, leeks	carrots, parsnips, beetroot

A handy way to remember this plan is using the mnemonic 'People Love Bunches Of Roses'.

WHAT ABOUT THE OTHER VEGETABLES?
Of course, there are lots of other vegetables that don't fit in any of these groups, like lettuce, courgettes and pumpkins. We grow these pretty much anywhere there's space.

I DON'T HAVE FIVE SEPARATE BEDS!
If you don't have five veg beds, don't worry! You can just divide the one bed you have into five areas. And if you're growing in containers, you don't have to worry about crop rotation at all!

LIGHT
With one or two exceptions, most veg plants love sunlight, so try and put your veg patch where it will get lots of sun. Veg grown in the shade will be just very, very sad.

SHELTER
A bit like me, veg plants don't like the wind (unless it's a gentle breeze on a hot summer's day). Having a bit of shelter for your veg patch (trees, hedge, fencing, etc.) will help them grow happy.

TREES
Don't put your veg patch too near trees. If you spend lots of time getting lots of nutrition into your veg patch, the trees will figure that out and send their roots in there to snaffle it up! Don't forget that the roots of a tree can be as deep as

WATER
Make sure there is a water source nearby, like a hose or water butt. Otherwise, you will end up with long arms like me from carrying watering cans all over the garden.

EAT

HANDY SPROUT HACK
If you're boiling or steaming your sprouts, remember to cut an X in the bottom of them beforehand to make sure they cook through.

HERB HERO

FENNEL

Did you know?
Fennel leaf has a very distinctive smell and an almost liquorice-like taste. You can eat the whole thing: the seeds, bulb, stalk, and leaves. It's used as a vegetable, a herb and a spice. You can brew fennel in hot water to make your own fennel tea, use the crunchy bulb in salads, or use the stalks for making soups. The Greek word for fennel is *marathon*. The Ancient Greeks believed that fennel helped your bones, which could make you fit enough to run a marathon, I suppose ... Fennel helps digestion and eases wind. In the past, people gave fennel syrup to babies with colic, to ease their windy tummies.

When to sow?
We sow fennel indoors in small pots from March onwards. In early summer, plant out into larger pots or into the soil in a sunny spot.

How to grow?
Fennel is a perennial which means it lasts for many years. Harvest the leaves as you need them. The plant gets lovely yellow flowers in the summer.

Tasty in:

curry ← Salad ← ← FISH SOUP

POULTRY

WHAT'S IN December SEASON

PARSNIPS
Want a tasty root vegetable tray for Christmas Day? Mix your parsnips with carrots and red onion and roast them at 180°C with a little oil, thyme and balsamic vinegar for 24 minutes.

SPROUTS
Look to the next page for ideas that will change even the fussiest eater's mind about sprouts.

CELERIAC
Roast celeriac with a little oil, salt and pepper for a great side dish to pair with poultry and fish.

KALE
See p. 13 for ways to use up your kale crop.

chARD
Tossed in a pan with salt, pepper and oil or butter, this vegetable doesn't need much cooking but is a great winter staple.

100

SPROUT HASH

makes enough for 4

If you have any sprouts that you didn't use on Christmas Day, why not use them to make a sprout hash for breakfast? This recipe is also a great way to use up leftover potatoes.

Wash Brussels sprouts (400g).

Remove any loose leaves.

Grate the sprouts into a bowl using a coarse grater. It should look like shredded cabbage.

Chop a shallot (1).

Heat oil (2 tbsp) in a frying pan.

HELPING HAND

Cook your shallot for 2–3 minutes.

Add your shredded sprouts to the pan and fry them up for 2–3 minutes.

Crumble in some **leftover cooked potatoes** (4 large) and cook until crispy.

Season the hash with salt and pepper.

Serve with **toast** and a poached or fried **egg** for a post-Christmas breakfast feast!

The NOT-SO-GREAT POETRY CORNER

HONEY-ROASTED SPROUTS

makes enough for 4

& as a side dish

I think sprouts are the sweetest little veg I know, cute little mini cabbage cousins that they are! But what if they actually tasted sweet too? They can! I like to roast mine with honey for the sweetest sprouts you've ever tasted. I've even managed to convert some bah humbug sprout haters with this recipe.

HELPING HAND

Wash some Brussels sprouts (500g).

Slice the stem off your sprouts and cut them in half.

Place them on a baking tray.

Mix oil (2 tbsp), **Balsamic vinegar** (2 tbsp) and **Honey** (2 tbsp), then drizzle over the sprouts in the tray.

Season with salt and pepper.

Bake for 20 minutes at 200°C, shaking them around in their tray after 10 minutes to make sure all sides get baked evenly.

Serve with a roast dinner!

IT'S A HARD SPROUT LIFE

Sick to his back teeth of being loved or loathed,
Russell the Sprout felt discommoded,
All the time trying too hard to please,
Never as popular as garden peas.

People making jokes about sprouts being smelly,
Debates in newspapers and on the telly,
Being overcooked in boiling water,
Being pushed around the plate by someone's daughter.

Being tolerated at Christmas, or considered quirky,
Piled high on a plate beside the turkey,
Even then not getting a smack of the lips,
Playing second fiddle to carrots or parsnips.

But one thing hurt Russell with great severity,
A fellow brassica's growing celebrity.
With sprouts dismissed as 'cabbage that's bendy',
How come kale is seen as trendy?

'Enough' said Russell from the fridge's bottom shelf,
'I need to go off and discover myself.'
To India he travelled, spent time in an ashram,
Lived off grid, didn't even send a telegram.

Did yoga, learnt to knit, considered joining the circus,
Found happiness and felt he'd rediscovered his purpose,
Proud to be on your plate, being good for your heart,
Comfortable with the fact that sprouts make you fart.

What Russell SPROUT Did Next...

Hi Monty

I know you're not a fan of air miles anymore, but I decided to go off on my travels to find myself. I presume you noticed I was gone. I've been having fun and enclose some pics to show you what I've been up to. I'm staying away until after Christmas at least just to be on the safe side. How's the kale doing? Say hi to Garlic Mick and all at GROW HQ.

Your friend, Russell.

MONTY POTTS
POTTING SH
COUNTY
ÉIRE

I took a trip to my hometown — Brussels, Belgium

I ran my first marathon. (see — told you I was healthy!)

I saw the pyramids of Giza, and met a very hungry camel.

ABOUT THE (OTHER) AUTHORS

Michael (or Garlic Mick as Monty calls him) started GIY and loves to talk and write about growing food. He presents a TV series called *Grow Cook Eat* and has written books about food growing. When not telling his garlic story (over and over again, to anyone who will listen), Michael can be found down the end of his garden pondering his compost heap. He's obsessed with growing tomatoes and this year planted over eighty plants. From July to September he is often to be found up to his neck in tomatoes in the kitchen trying to make the perfect passata. He once recorded an album called *Amongst Women* which nobody bought (except his mum). He lives in Dunmore East with his wife, two avid young GIYers, and an ever-expanding coterie of farmyard animals.

Muireann is a writer and TV performer who *loves* food. You can often see her hanging about with some of her favourite vegetables or presenting cookery or food quiz shows. She loves a good food fact, but don't depend on her in a table quiz, her handwriting is very messy! Her favourite colour is yellow and so is her favourite fruit. According to Muireann, the lemon is 'the unsung hero of the kitchen'. She's not a chef but spends all her free time cooking and experimenting in the kitchen at home and testing her recipes out on her family. She likes thinking up wacky ways of using up her leftovers and has been known to make some pretty unusual sandwiches – apple and cheese is her current favourite.

Fatti is an illustrator from Dunmore East who loves to draw pictures of the things that interest her the most – animals, funny incidents and interesting people. Food just happens to be her favourite thing of all time! She loves cooking (almost as much as she loves eating) and got her interest in gardening from her father John, who always had an impressive vegetable patch in their back garden. She has been illustrating non-fiction books for children since 2015 and finds that she's most inspired when she's learning new things. When she's not drawing at her desk, she's trying some new hobby or travelling with her partner Acky and their dog Aidan, trying new and exciting recipes from around the world.

DEDICATIONS

Mick would like to thank all the team at GIY and GROW HQ who live the 'grow, cook, eat' ethos each and every day. He would like to thank Muireann, Fatti and Stephen Kelly for taking a leap of faith and jumping on board with this project from day one; and Liz Hudson for helping us to dot the is and cross the ts. Above all he thanks his wife Eilish and his two children Nicky and Vika who were the inspiration for writing this book – he hopes they keep on growing, use the recipes and laugh at the jokes.

Muireann would like to thank all the youngsters she has met through her work over the years, especially the budding young gardeners and chefs for inspiring her to write a book like this. This book is yours, use it well. She would like to thank Mick and GIY for taking a chance on a wild idea. She dedicates this book to her family: her husband John who put up with some interesting recipes along the way and her young son Tommaí who she hopes won't be a picky eater and will grow up to have greener fingers than Monty.

Fatti would like to dedicate this b ook to her nephews Kevin, Sean and Finn, and her nieces Neeta and Rosa; to her parents, whos gardens have always been a haven; and to Acky for always sharing his food with her.

How many times did you see me in the book?

ANSWER = sawit LS